Non-Latin typefaces

at St Bride Library, London and Department of Typography & Graphic Communication, University of Reading

Detail from Tibetan astrological chart, early twentieth-century [courtesy Fiona Ross].

Non-Latin typefaces

In September 2007 a two-day conference on the subject of non-Latin typeface design was held at the St Bride Library, London, and at the Department of Typography & Graphic Communication, University of Reading. This was accompanied by substantial exhibitions on the theme of the conference from the collections of both institutions, much of which had rarely been seen before and not in such a concentrated manner. A small number of items that augmented the exhibits at Reading were loaned from private collections. The exhibitions were curated by Fiona Ross and Rathna Ramanathan; the St Bride exhibition was also co-curated by Jo De Baerdemaeker.

This book shows a selection from the exhibits displayed in both venues prefaced with essays by James Mosley and Fiona Ross describing the rich collections from which the exhibits were drawn; the St Bride Library and the Linotype Non-Latin Collection at the University of Reading respectively.

Harry Carter, sketch of Russian characters for Monotype Series 169 R.

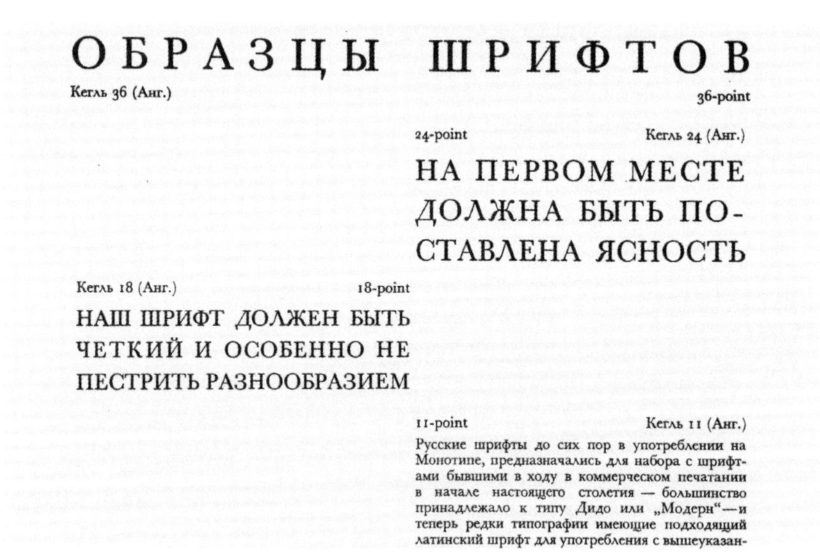

ОБРАЗЦЫ ШРИФТОВ

Кегль 36 (Анг.) 36-point

24-point Кегль 24 (Анг.)

НА ПЕРВОМ МЕСТЕ ДОЛЖНА БЫТЬ ПОСТАВЛЕНА ЯСНОСТЬ

Кегль 18 (Анг.) 18-point

НАШ ШРИФТ ДОЛЖЕН БЫТЬ ЧЕТКИЙ И ОСОБЕННО НЕ ПЕСТРИТЬ РАЗНООБРАЗИЕМ

11-point Кегль 11 (Анг.)

Русские шрифты до сих пор в употреблении на Монотипе, предназначались для набора с шрифтами бывшими в ходу в коммерческом печатании в начале настоящего столетия — большинство принадлежало к типу Дидо или „Модерн"—и теперь редки типографии имеющие подходящий латинский шрифт для употребления с вышеуказан-

A specimen of a New Russian Type Monotype Series 169 R, 1932 (detail 130 × 211 mm).

St Bride Library, London

James Mosley is Visiting Professor in the Department of Typography & Graphic Communication at the University of Reading, and writes and lectures on the history of type and letterforms. He was Librarian of the St Bride Library from 1958 until 2000.

The St Bride Library owes the special qualities of its collections to a series of separate events at the time of its establishment. During the late 1880s, several parish charities that had become obsolete were consolidated into the 'St Bride Foundation'. The technology of printing had become so complex that it was recognized that conventional apprenticeship needed to be supplemented by formal instruction at a trade school, so training in letterpress and lithographic printing was provided in the new St Bride Foundation Institute building. And in April 1890, William Blades, a printer in the City of London who had spent many years writing his study of the life and work of William Caxton, died at his house at Sutton, to the south of London.

Blades had built up a remarkable personal library, comprising not only works on the history of printing and publishing but also the practical manuals of printing and related technologies, and even the catalogues of manufacturers of materials for printing. In 1863 he had written in a trade paper, the *Printer's Register*, of the value of making a collection of typefounders' specimens, which as catalogues of goods for sale were largely ignored by major libraries. With the help of a fund set up for the purpose, the library was bought and installed in the building of the new Institute, and opened in 1895.

Blades had taken a leading role in the 'Caxton celebration' of 1877, an exhibition to mark the four hundred years since the installation of Caxton's press at Westminster, at which the printer's tools and type specimens were on display. He fired a young typefounder, Talbot Baines Reed, with his own enthusiasm for the literature of printing, and Reed wrote what is still the most important document for the history of type in Britain, his *History of the old English letter foundries* (1887). When Reed died prematurely, his own library, complementing that of Blades and including many type specimens, was also bought for the St Bride Foundation. These special collections, and some others too, were installed in the new Technical Library that was designed for the use of the teachers and students of the printing school.

One further event determined the future shape of the library. After the First World War the London County Council, which had been paying the larger part of the costs of the 'Technical School', took it away and set it up as the 'London School of Printing' in a building of its own (it later became the London College of Printing and the London College of Communication). The Governing Body of the Foundation refused to let the library follow the school, and so it remained at the Institute in Bride Lane. There were disadvantages in this loss of funding, a handicap that the library has suffered from for most of its existence, and also in the layout of the building. But there were two advantages. A working technical library tends to discard obsolete materials, and those that are in intensive use are worn to pieces. Some books that can now be found in the St Bride collection – a hypothetical example might be the fifth edition of a standard work which gives a valuable picture of the state of the technology of printing at a specific moment – now exist nowhere else. The other positive effect was to make the library a natural place of deposit by the printing trade and its suppliers. The London office of the Monotype Corporation was within a few minutes' walk from Bride Lane. Many of its employees, including Stanley Morison, treated St Brides as if it was a lending library created for their benefit. But in return, they made sure – in common with other members of the trade – that it received all the new publications. The donation of the papers of Harry Carter, typographic designer and historian of type, from which the sketches for the Cyrillic characters added to Monotype's Baskerville to make Series 169R are shown above, are evidence of this affection felt by members of 'the trade' for the St Bride collection that has been demonstrated countless times.

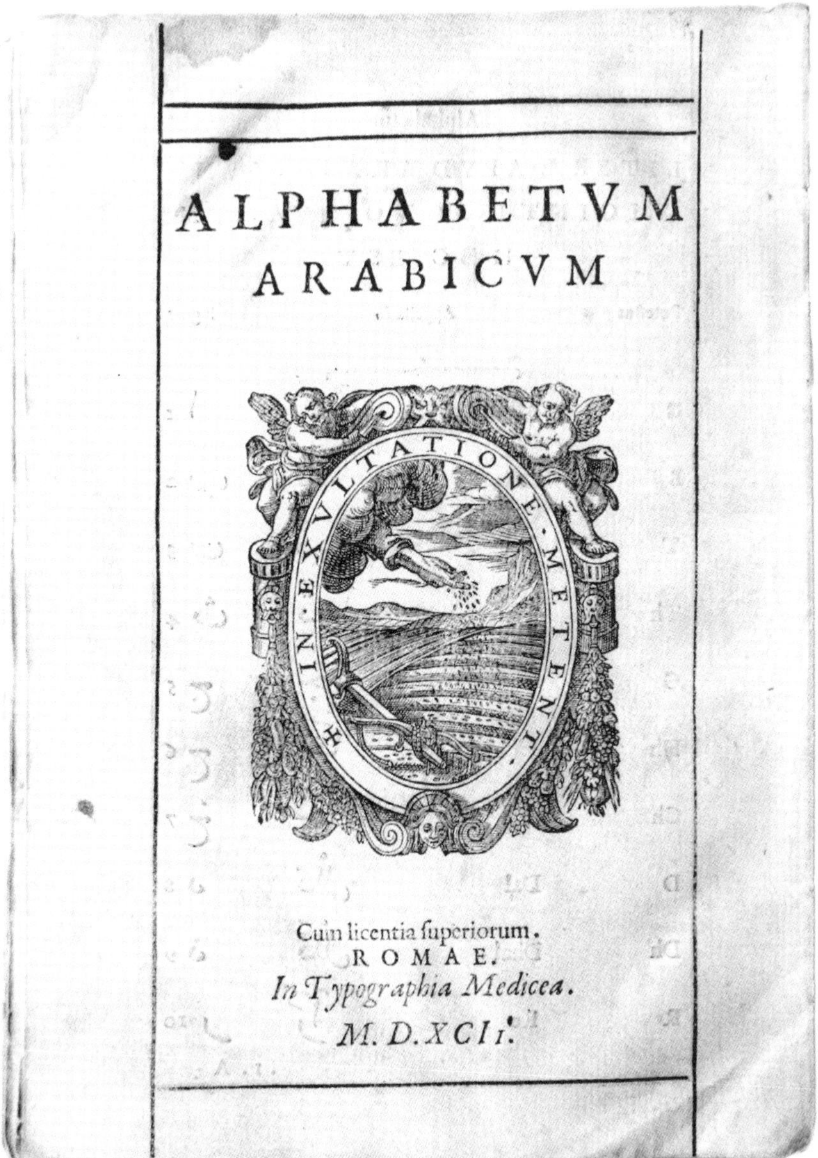

ALPHABETVM
ARABICVM

IN·EXVLTATIONE·METENT·

Cum licentia superiorum.
ROMAE.
In Typographia Medicea.
M.D.XCII.

Alphabetum arabicum, Rome: Typographia Medicea, 1592. 215 × 155 mm.

Exercitatio 64

في البدء كان الكلمة و الكلمة كان عند الله و الله
هو الكلمة كان هذا قديما عند الله كل به كان
و بغيره لم يكن شي مما كان به كانت الحياة و الحياة
هي نور الناس و النور اضاء في الظلمة و الظلمة لم
تدركه كان انسان ارسل من الله اسمه يوحنا هذا
جاء للشهادة ليشهد للنور ليومن الكل به و لم يكن
هو النور بل ليشهد للنور الذي هو نور الحق الذي
يضي لكل انسان ات

Phil-badi kanal-kalemato, ual-kalemato kana indal-lahi, ual-laho houal-kalemato . kana hadha qadiman indal-lahi . kollo behi kana, ua beghairihi lam iakon ſciaiion mimma kana . behi kanatil-hhaiato, ual-hhaiato hia nuron-naſi, uan-nuro adhaa phitdh-tdholmati, uatdhtdholmato lam todrekho . kana enſanon orſela menal-lahismoho iuhanna . hadha giaa lilſcſciahadati leiaſchada lilnuri leiaumenal-kollo behi, ua lam iakon houan-nura, bal leiaſchada lilnuril-ladhi houa nurol-hhaqqol ladhi iodhion lekolli anſanin atin . Hoc eſt .

In principio erat uerbum, & uerbum erat apud Deum & Deus erat uerbum, erat hoc in principio apud Deum omnia per ipſum facta ſunt & ſine ipſo factum eſt nihil eorum quæ facta ſunt . In ipſo erat uita, & uita erat lux hominum & lux lucet in tenebris, & tenebræ non cōprehenderunt eam. Fuit homo miſſus à Deo, cuius nomen erat Iohannes . hic uenit in teſtimonium ut teſtimoniū perhiberet de lumine, ut crederēt omnes per illū . Et nō fuit ille lux, ſed ut teſtimonium perhiberet de lumine, quod eſt lux uera, quæ illuminat omnem hominem ue nientē, & cæt :

Arabic types cut by Robert Ganjon, *Alphabetum arabicum*, Rome: Typographia Medicea, 1592. 215 × 155 mm.

The period about which I can write from my own experience has been a no less problematic one for the library than those that it followed. It seems a trivial matter, but until a relatively recent date, when the idea was quietly dropped, the postwar plan of the City of London provided for a street to be driven between St Bride's Church and the Institute. If it had been built this would have led to the demolition of the Institute. (The curious kink in the east-west part of Bride Lane is a legacy from this abortive plan.) One result of this threat was the neglect of the long term maintenance of the structure, but another was the relative tolerance of the Governing body of the use by the library of additional areas within a building that seemed to have so short a life, and this greatly helped in the building of the collections during this period. The most positive single development, albeit one with a limited term, began in 1966, when the St Bride Library was brought within the library system of the City of London, and not only began to make up for the books it had been unable to buy, but to make some serious additions to the libraries of Blades and Reed in the spirit of their own collecting. The quarto *Alphabetum arabicum* (1592) of the Typographia Medicea, a missionary press in Rome, showing one of the Arabic types specially cut for it by Robert Granjon, will stand as just one example among many of the kind of purchase that has enhanced the collection and which would have been unthinkable during the years between 1920 and 1966.

The other development since the 1960s that is shown in the library's present collections has been the result of the changing technology of printing, awareness of which was demonstrated at the exhibition 'Printing and the mind of man' in 1963 and the founding of the Printing Historical Society and related groups in other countries. Aware of the value of preserving at least some artefacts of printing, as well as books, the library added a working printing office and types, and provided space for some typographical materials that related directly to its existing holdings of type specimens, but which would almost certainly have been destroyed without its intervention. The punches and matrices of the Figgins foundry, together with specimens, synopses and case lays of non-Latin types from the same source, is one example, as are the many non-Latin founts of type in case from the University Press at Oxford.

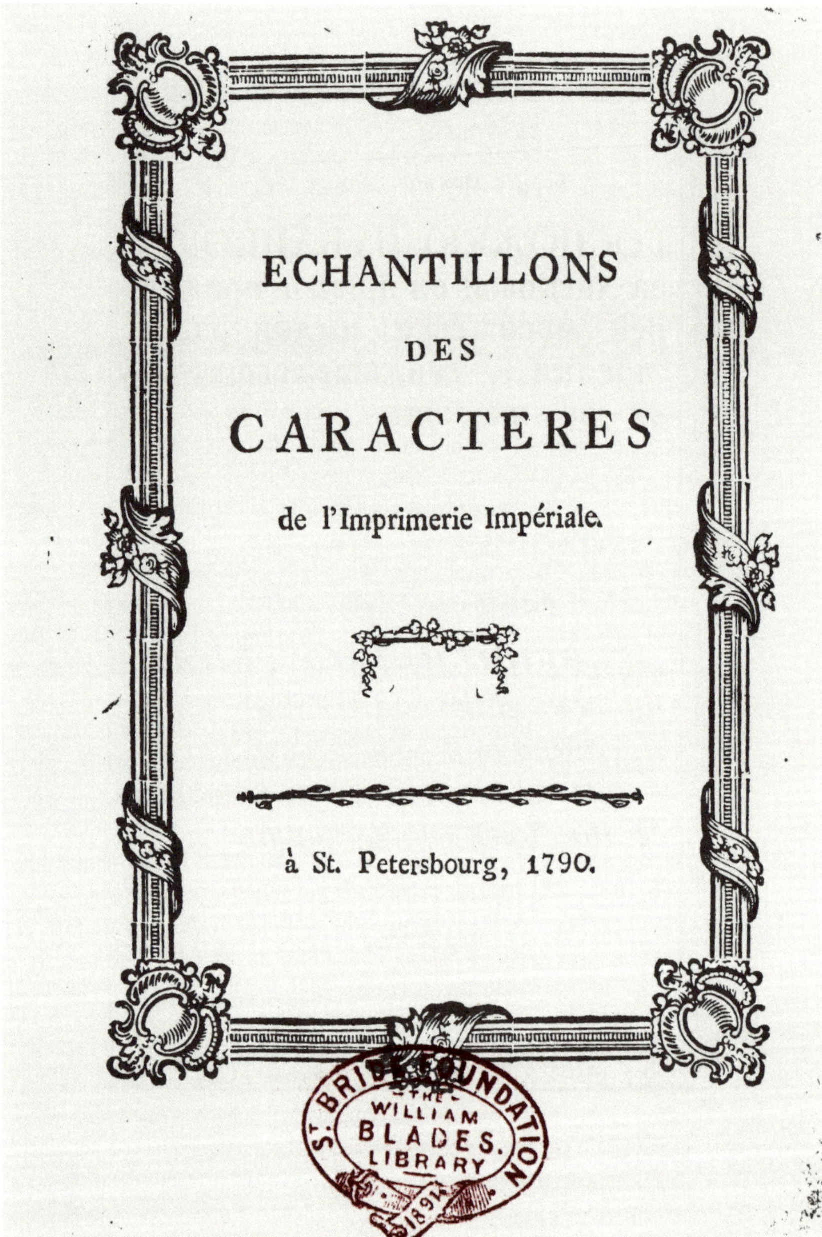

ECHANTILLONS

DES

CARACTERES

de l'Imprimerie Impériale.

à St. Petersbourg, 1790.

Échantillons des caractères de l'Imprimerie Impériale, St Petersburg: l'Imprimerie Impériale, 1790. Title page (above) and specimen page of Cyrillic types (right). 192 × 123 mm.

Терція Прямой. No. 7. *M.*

ГОСПОЖЕЮ ПУБЛИКОЮ
за ласковой ея пріемъ преж-
ней моей сего имяни те-
традки, свидѣтельствуя
ей за то отъ 1 2 3 4 5

Терція Курзивъ. No. 8. *M.*

*ИСКРЕННѢЙШАГО СЕРД-
ца всю мою благодарность,
постараюсь отслужить
сколько могу, тѣмъ чтобы
ее по долѣ позабавить*

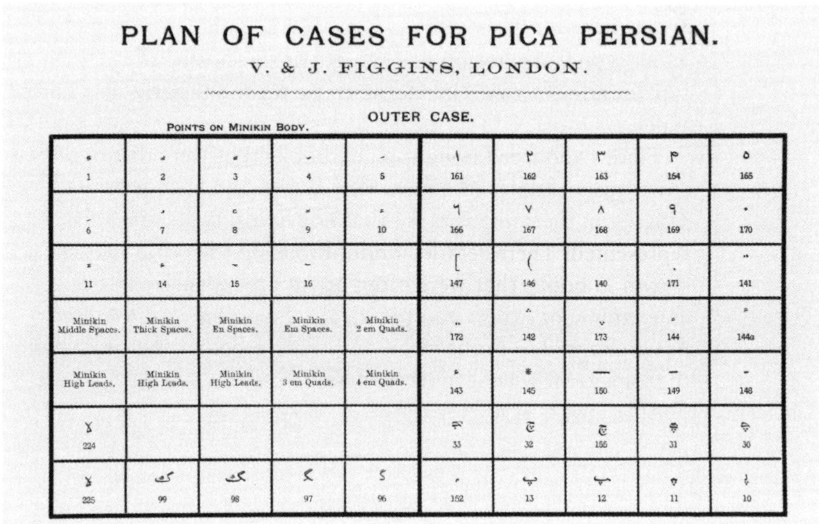

Plan of cases for Pica Persian, outer case, London: Vincent Figgins, *c* 1880 (detail 130 × 210 mm).

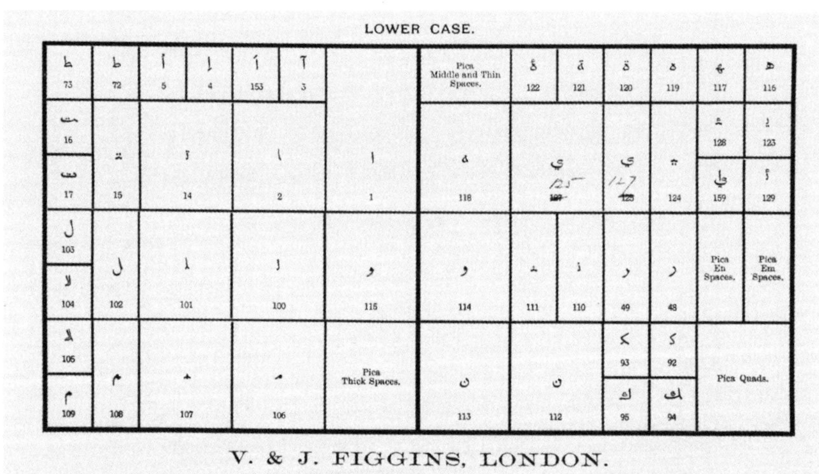

Plan of cases for Pica Persian, lower case, London: Vincent Figgins, *c* 1880 (detail 115 × 210 mm).

The University Press also passed over the punches that the Monotype Corporation had bought at the closing of the Caslon typefoundry in 1936, including those for many early non-Latin types.

Blades and Reed bought many books that were distinguished chiefly as examples of noteworthy types, and both were wide-ranging in their interests, so that non-Latin types are well represented. Their detailed annotations on the types that are shown in books that were often not at all expensive to buy set an example of expert and practical scholarship that the library has attempted to profit from, and to develop in other ways, for the long-term benefit of its readers.

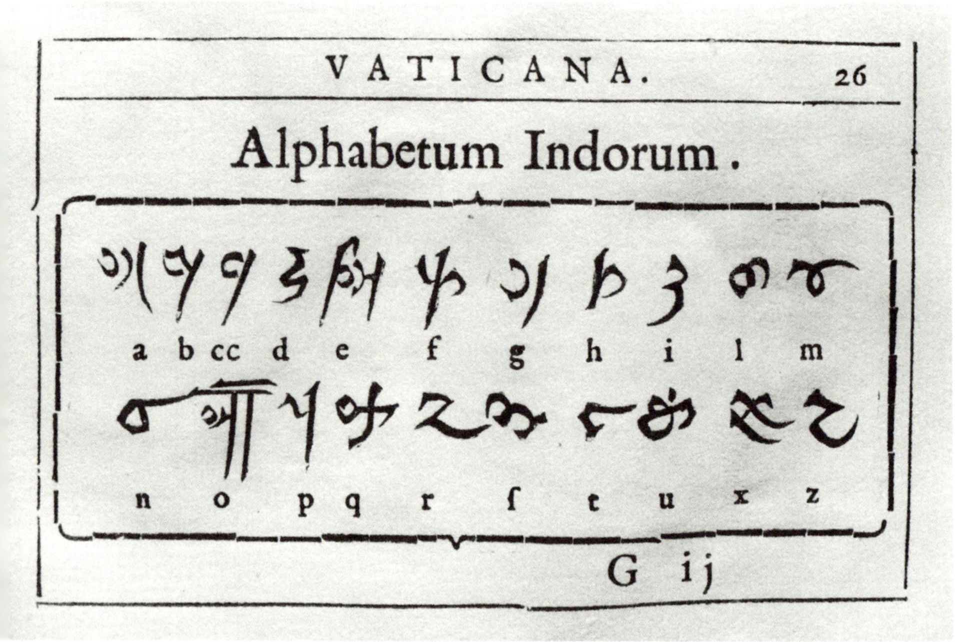

SB 1 'Alphabetum Indorum': *Indice de caratteri, con l'inventori, e nomi di essi esistenti nella stampa Vaticana e Camerale*, Rome: Stamperia Vaticana, 1628 (detail 72 × 116 mm).

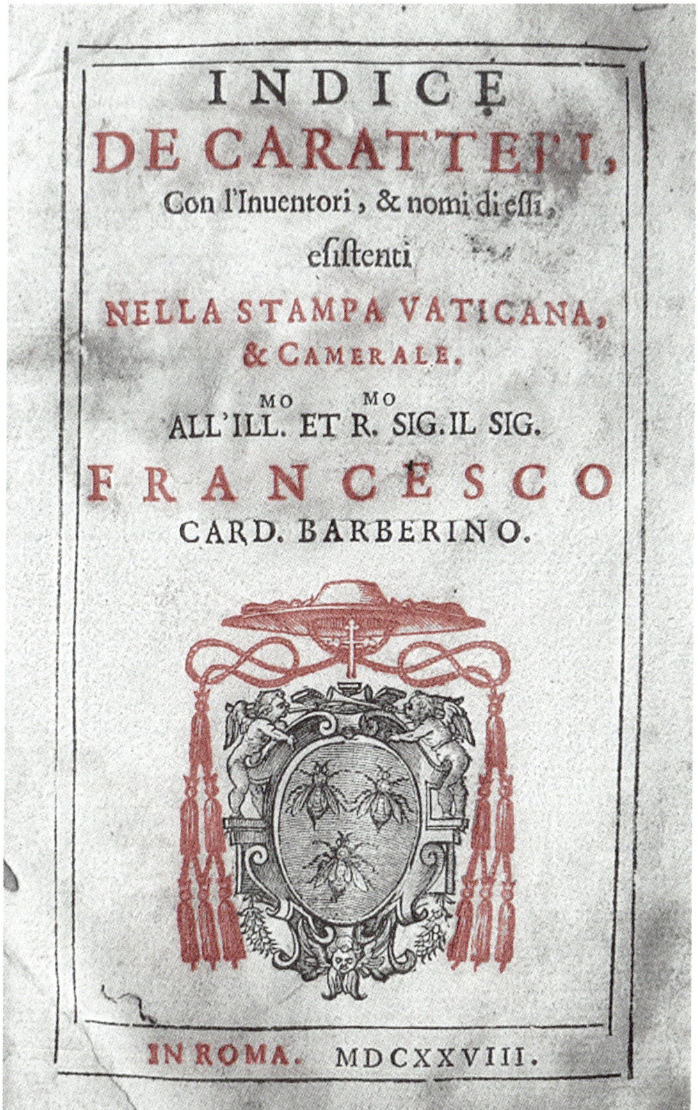
INDICE
DE CARATTERI,
Con l'Inuentori, & nomi di essi,
esistenti
NELLA STAMPA VATICANA,
& CAMERALE.
ALL'ILL.MO ET R.MO SIG. IL SIG.
FRANCESCO
CARD. BARBERINO.

IN ROMA. MDCXXVIII.

SB **2** *Indice de caratteri, con l'inventori, e nomi di essi esistenti nella stampa Vaticana e Camerale*, Rome: Stamperia Vaticana, 1628. 192 × 125 mm.

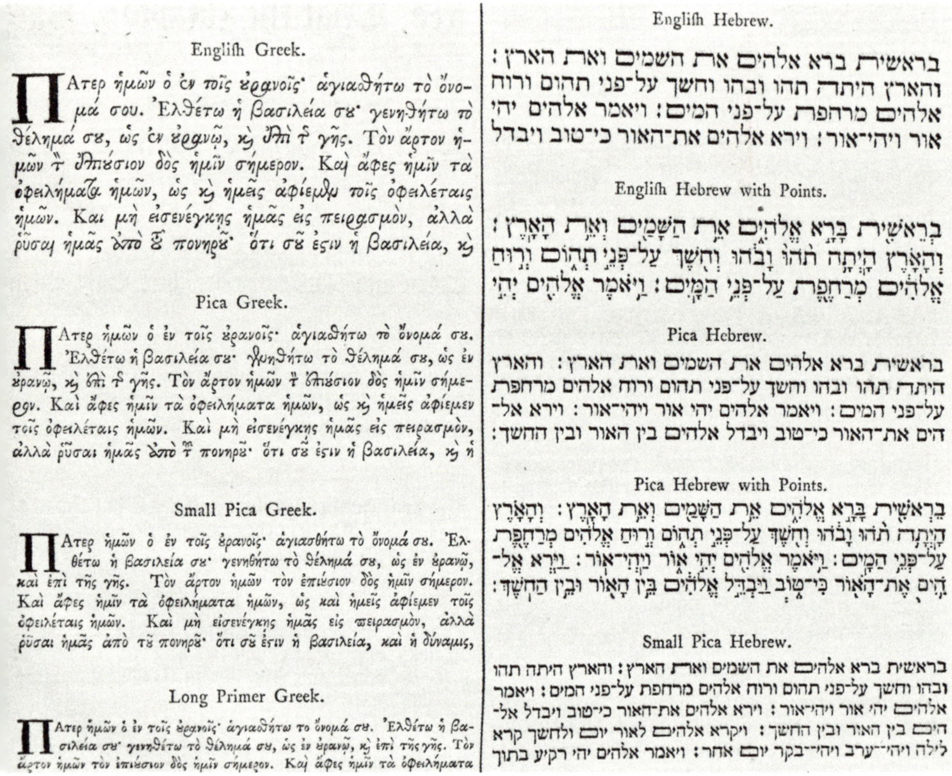

English Greek.

ΠΑτερ ἡμῶν ὁ ἐν τοῖς ȣ̓ρανοῖς· ἁγιασθήτω τὸ ὄνομά σου. Ἐλθέτω ἡ βασιλεία σȣ· γενηθήτω τὸ θέλημά σȣ, ὡς ἐν ȣ̓ρανῷ, καὶ ἐπὶ τῆς γῆς. Τὸν ἄρτον ἡμῶν τὸν ἐπιȣ́σιον δὸς ἡμῖν σήμερον. Καὶ ἄφες ἡμῖν τὰ ὀφειλήματα ἡμῶν, ὡς καὶ ἡμεῖς ἀφίεμεν τοῖς ὀφειλέταις ἡμῶν. Και μὴ εἰσενέγκῃς ἡμᾶς εἰς πειρασμὸν, ἀλλὰ ῥῦσαι ἡμᾶς ἀπὸ τȣ̃ πονηρȣ̃· ὅτι σȣ̃ ἐςιν ἡ βασιλεία, καὶ

Pica Greek.

ΠΑτερ ἡμῶν ὁ ἐν τοῖς ȣ̓ρανοῖς· ἁγιασθήτω τὸ ὄνομά σȣ. Ἐλθέτω ἡ βασιλεία σȣ· γενηθήτω τὸ θέλημά σȣ, ὡς ἐν ȣ̓ρανῷ, καὶ ἐπὶ τῆς γῆς. Τὸν ἄρτον ἡμῶν τὸν ἐπιȣ́σιον δὸς ἡμῖν σήμερον. Καὶ ἄφες ἡμῖν τὰ ὀφειλήματα ἡμῶν, ὡς καὶ ἡμεῖς ἀφίεμεν τοῖς ὀφειλέταις ἡμῶν. Καὶ μὴ εἰσενέγκῃς ἡμᾶς εἰς πειρασμὸν, ἀλλὰ ῥῦσαι ἡμᾶς ἀπὸ τȣ̃ πονηρȣ̃· ὅτι σȣ̃ ἐςιν ἡ βασιλεία, καὶ ἡ

Small Pica Greek.

ΠΑτερ ἡμῶν ὁ ἐν τοῖς ȣ̓ρανοῖς· ἁγιασθήτω τὸ ὄνομά σȣ. Ἐλθέτω ἡ βασιλεία σȣ· γενηθήτω τὸ θέλημά σȣ, ὡς ἐν ȣ̓ρανῷ, καὶ ἐπὶ τῆς γῆς. Τὸν ἄρτον ἡμῶν τὸν ἐπιȣ́σιον δὸς ἡμῖν σήμερον. Καὶ ἄφες ἡμῖν τὰ ὀφειλήματα ἡμῶν, ὡς καὶ ἡμεῖς ἀφίεμεν τοῖς ὀφειλέταις ἡμῶν. Καὶ μὴ εἰσενέγκῃς ἡμᾶς εἰς πειρασμὸν, ἀλλὰ ῥῦσαι ἡμᾶς ἀπὸ τȣ̃ πονηρȣ̃· ὅτι σȣ̃ ἐςιν ἡ βασιλεία, καὶ ἡ δύναμις,

Long Primer Greek.

ΠΑτερ ἡμῶν ὁ ἐν τοῖς ȣ̓ρανοῖς· ἁγιασθήτω το ὄνομά σȣ. Ἐλθέτω ἡ βασιλεία σȣ· γενηθέτω τὸ θέλημά σȣ, ὡς ἐν ȣ̓ρανῷ, καὶ ἐπὶ τῆς γῆς. Τὸν ἄρτον ἡμῶν τὸν ἐπιȣ́σιον δὸς ἡμῖν σήμερον. Καὶ ἄφες ἡμῖν τὰ ὀφειλήματα

English Hebrew.

בראשית ברא אלהים את השמים ואת הארץ : והארץ היתה תהו ובהו וחשך על־פני תהום ורוח אלהים מרחפת על־פני המים : ויאמר אלהים יהי אור ויהי־אור : וירא אלהים את־האור כי־טוב ויבדל

English Hebrew with Points.

בְּרֵאשִׁית בָּרָא אֱלֹהִים אֵת הַשָּׁמַיִם וְאֵת הָאָרֶץ : וְהָאָרֶץ הָיְתָה תֹהוּ וָבֹהוּ וְחֹשֶׁךְ עַל־פְּנֵי תְהוֹם וְרוּחַ אֱלֹהִים מְרַחֶפֶת עַל־פְּנֵי הַמָּיִם : וַיֹּאמֶר אֱלֹהִים יְהִי

Pica Hebrew.

בראשית ברא אלהים את השמים ואת הארץ : והארץ היתה תהו ובהו וחשך על־פני תהום ורוח אלהים מרחפת על־פני המים : ויאמר אלהים יהי אור ויהי־אור : וירא אל־הים את־האור כי־טוב ויבדל אלהים בין האור ובין החשך :

Pica Hebrew with Points.

בְּרֵאשִׁית בָּרָא אֱלֹהִים אֵת הַשָּׁמַיִם וְאֵת הָאָרֶץ : וְהָאָרֶץ הָיְתָה תֹהוּ וָבֹהוּ וְחֹשֶׁךְ עַל־פְּנֵי תְהוֹם וְרוּחַ אֱלֹהִים מְרַחֶפֶת עַל־פְּנֵי הַמָּיִם : וַיֹּאמֶר אֱלֹהִים יְהִי אוֹר וַיְהִי־אוֹר : וַיַּרְא אֱל־הִים אֶת־הָאוֹר כִּי־טוֹב וַיַּבְדֵּל אֱלֹהִים בֵּין הָאוֹר וּבֵין הַחֹשֶׁךְ :

Small Pica Hebrew.

בראשית ברא אלהים את השמים וארת הארץ : והארץ היתה תהו ובהו וחשך על־פני תהום ורוח אלהים מרחפת על־פני המים : ויאמר אלהים יהי אור ויהי־אור : וירא אלהים את־האור כי־טוב ויבדל אל־הים בין האור ובין החשך : ויקרא אלהים לאור יום ולחשך קרא לילה ויהי־ערב ויהי־בקר יום אחד : ויאמר אלהים יהי רקיע בתוך

SB 3 *A specimen of printing types*, London: William Caslon, 1785. 263 × 430 mm (detail 137 × 180 mm).

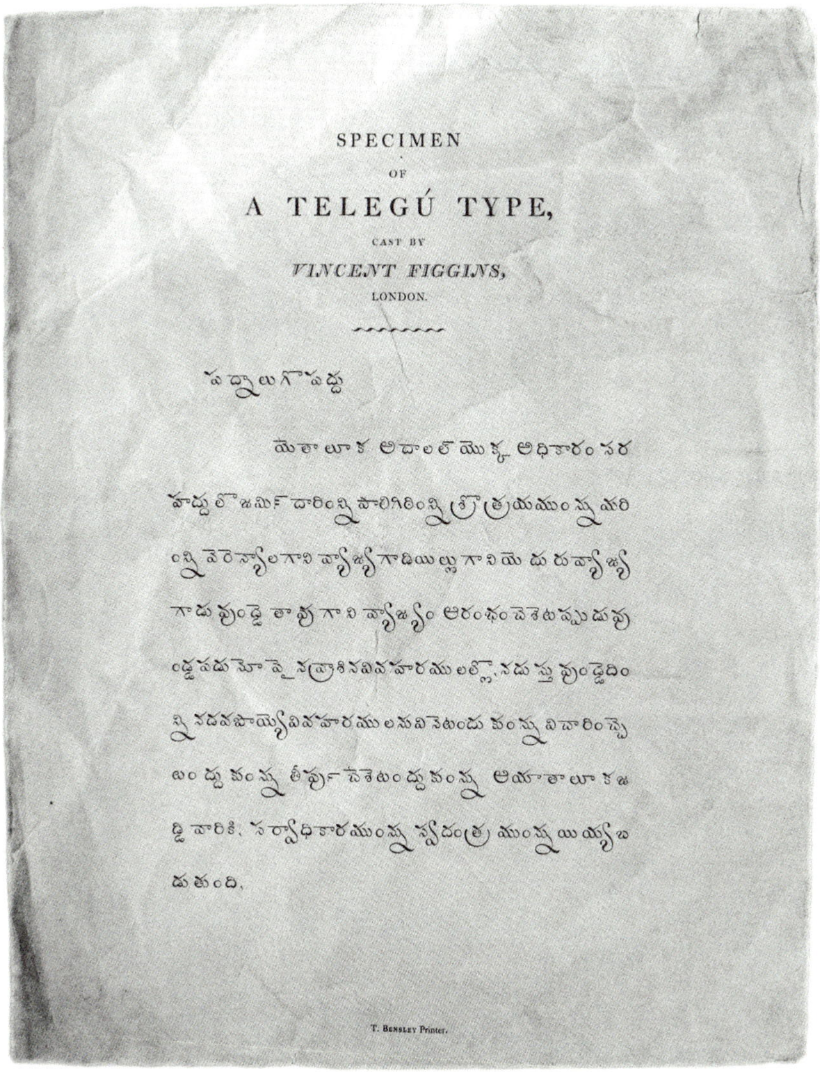

SPECIMEN

OF

A TELEGÚ TYPE,

CAST BY

VINCENT FIGGINS,

LONDON.

T. Bensley Printer.

SB 4 *Specimen of a Telugu type*, London: Vincent Figgins, 1802. 300 × 240 mm.

Alt-Cyrillisch, Böhmisch, Bulgarisch, Croatisch, Dänisch, Englisch, Französisch, Griechisch, Hebräisch, Holländisch, Italienisch.

Въ первомъ случаѣ пригодны всѣ правила титульнаго

Ние всички, било селяне или граждане, били хъ-

Природни је закон у животу народа да нови

Ние всички, било селяне или граждане,

Както всякому отъ, насъ се

Въ первомъ случаѣ пригодны всѣ правила титульнаго

Природни је закон у животу народа да нови

Ние всички, било селяне или граждане,

Νῦν δὲ πειρασόμεθα διηγήσασθαι, ὡς ἐπὶ

GEGRÜNDET 1856.

Schriftgiesserei

J. H. RUST & Co.

WIEN

V., GRIESGASSE 10.

GRÖSSTE AUSWAHL fremdsprachlicher Schriften.

EINRICHTUNG vollständiger Buchdruckereien.

והיה מספר בני־ישראל כחול הים אשר לא־ימד

לא־ימד ולא

בני־ישרא

השבת

На перкомъ, котрай мѣсто отъ

Баталіонъ Дорога

Врема Новые

Числомъ Молебствіе

Морошкинское Колмина

Іюль Сентябрь

КНЯЗЬ

Одинъ разъ дѣти

Календарь Новые

Polnisch, Portugiesisch, Rumänisch, Russisch, Ruthenisch, Serbisch, Slovakisch, Slovenisch, Spanisch, Schwedisch, Ungarisch.

SB 5 *Schriftgiesserei, J. H. Rust & Co*, Vienna: J. H. Rust & Co, 1856. 350 × 255 mm.

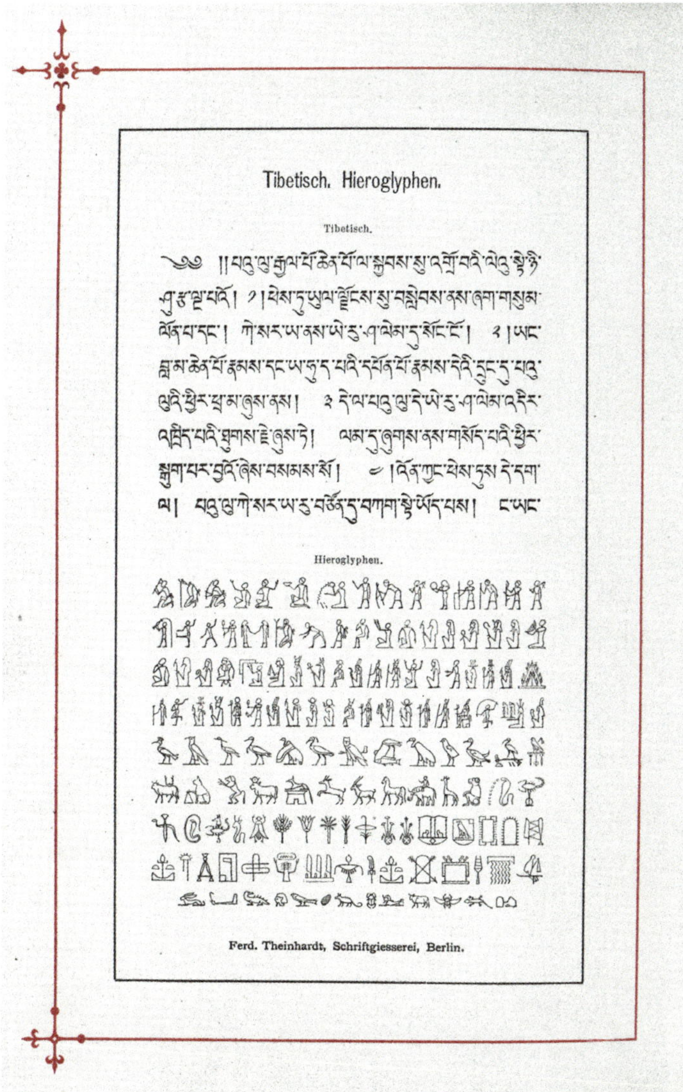

SB 6 Tibetan and Hieroglyphic in *Musterbuch*, Berlin: Schriftgiesserei Ferdinand Theinhardt, *c* 1895. 265 × 180 mm.

SB 7 Specimen of the Tokyo Tsukiji Type Foundry, printed in five colours, Tokyo: Tokyo Tsukiji Type Foundry, 1900. 543 × 710 mm.

氣銅版見本

◉以上掲クル所ハ新聞紙廣告用ヲ主トシテ新案セシ電氣銅版ニ御座候尚多種具ハリ居候間多少ニ拘ラス御注文願上候（紙中欄外番號ハ電氣銅版見本帳ノ番號金額ハ正價ニ御座候）

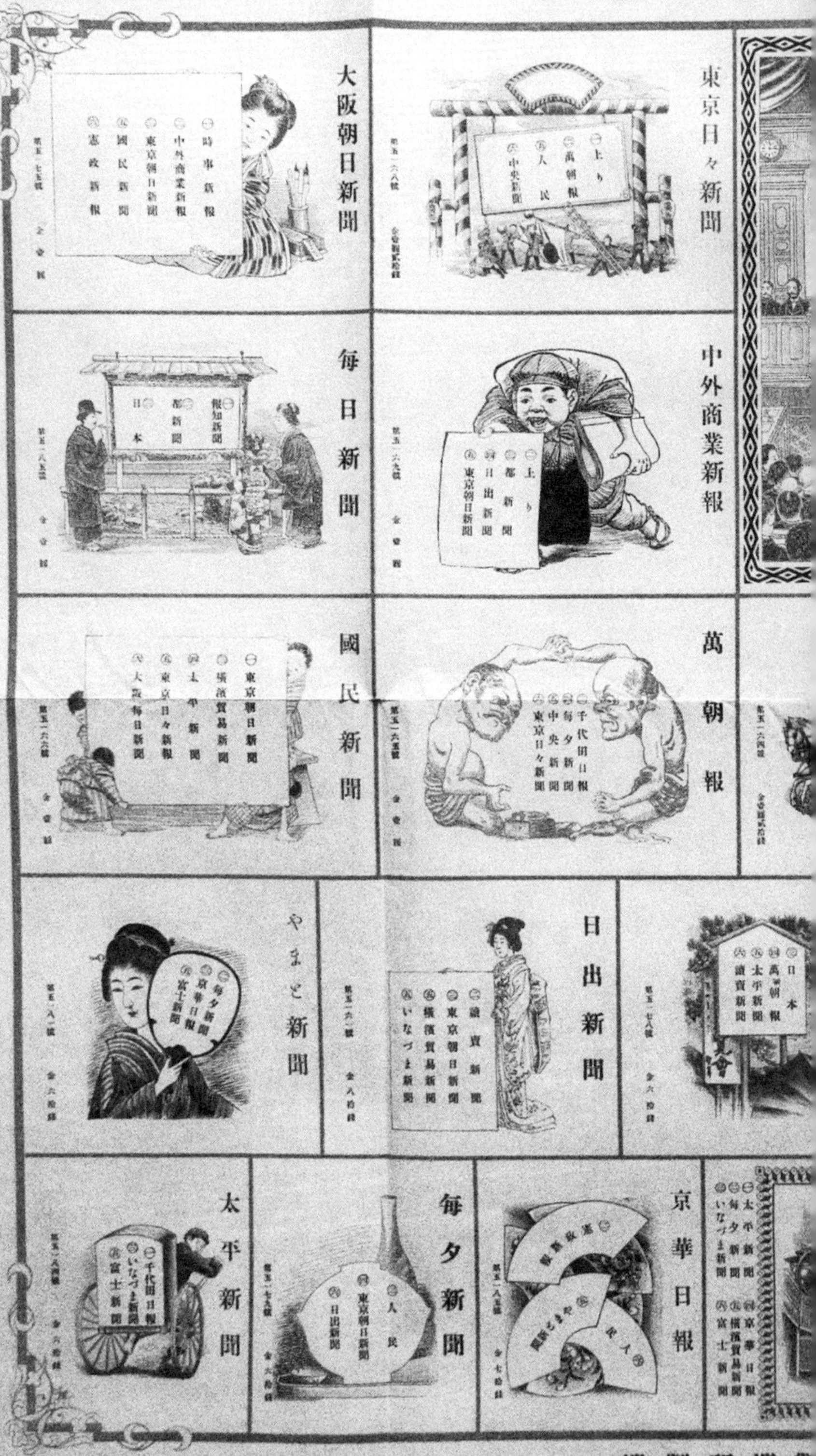

製造所製造

新聞紙廣告

新製見本第貳卷第四號附錄（明治三十三年一月發行）

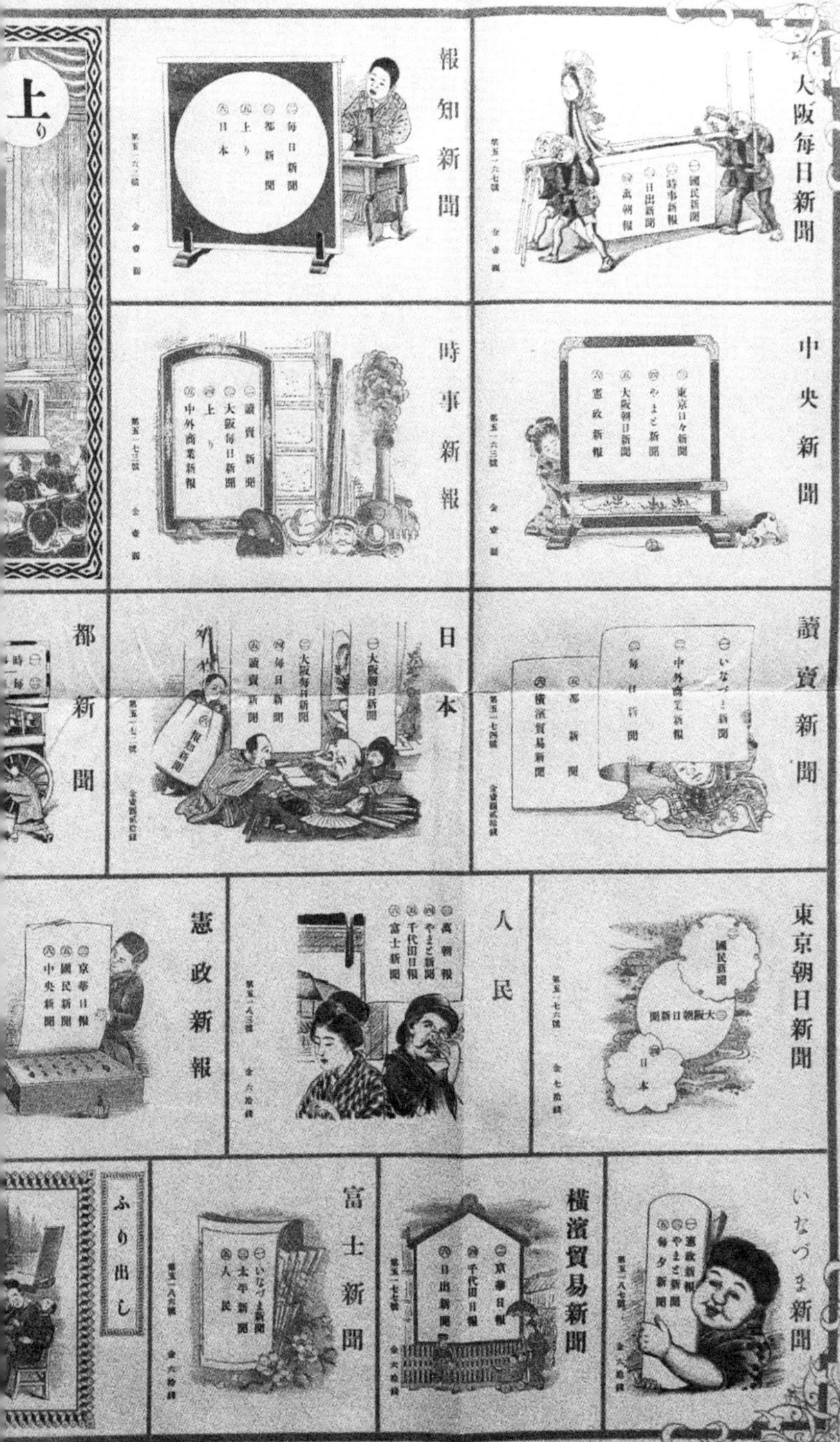

SB8 *Specimens of the Tokyo Tsukiji Type Foundry*, Tokyo: Tokyo Tsukiji Type Foundry, July 1897. 279 × 203 mm.

SB 9 Illustrated cover, *Reichsdrukerei Berlin*, Berlin, 1904. 168 × 250 mm.

SB 10 Specimen of Cyrillic typeface 'Korinna' from the 'Types and Ornaments' specimen book of H. Berthold Foundry, Moscow: H. Berthold Foundry, 1905. 331 × 248 mm (detail 278 × 203 mm).

SB 11 Buginese types in *Proeven van oostersche schriften*, Amsterdam: Lettergieterij Amsterdam, 1912. 261 × 190 mm.

Оригиналъ собственность словолитни.

КОРИННА

№ 1692. Кегль 16, мин. 20 фунт., за фунтъ 1 руб. 35 коп

Торговый Банкъ Ревель
Николай Пинесъ Emanuel Kant
ИМПЕРІЯ СОБРАНІЕ

№ 1693. Кегль 20, мин. 25 фунт., за фунтъ 1 руб. 30 коп.

Ледовитый океанъ
Объявленіе Memorandum
ИВАНЪ ЛЕВЪ

№ 1695. Кегль 28, мин. 30 фунт., за фунтъ 1 руб. 25 коп.

Шилово Павелъ Исаевъ Кисловка
HOHENAUE МЕЛЕНКИ

№ 1696. Кегль 36, мин. 35 фунт., за фунтъ 1 руб. 10 коп.

Кашино Kunst-Anstalt Ялама
ИВАНСКЪ BREMEN

№ 1697. Кегль 48, мин. 40 фунт., за фунтъ 1 руб. 5 коп.

Панино Nauhof Новки
RHEIN ЯПОНІЯ

Кромѣ французскихъ, есть польскія и др. акценти. буквы.

СЕМЕНЪ ВАЛДОВЪ ВАРШАВА

Складъ сельско-хозяйственныхъ машинъ

Искуственныя удобренія и разныя сѣмена

ПРЕДСТАВИТЕЛЬСТВО РУССКИХЪ И ЗАГРАНИЧНЫХЪ ЗАВОДОВЪ

Телефонъ № 2790 ▫ Невская улица № 25

Г. БЕРТГОЛЬДЪ, С.-ПЕТЕРБУРГЪ И МОСКВА

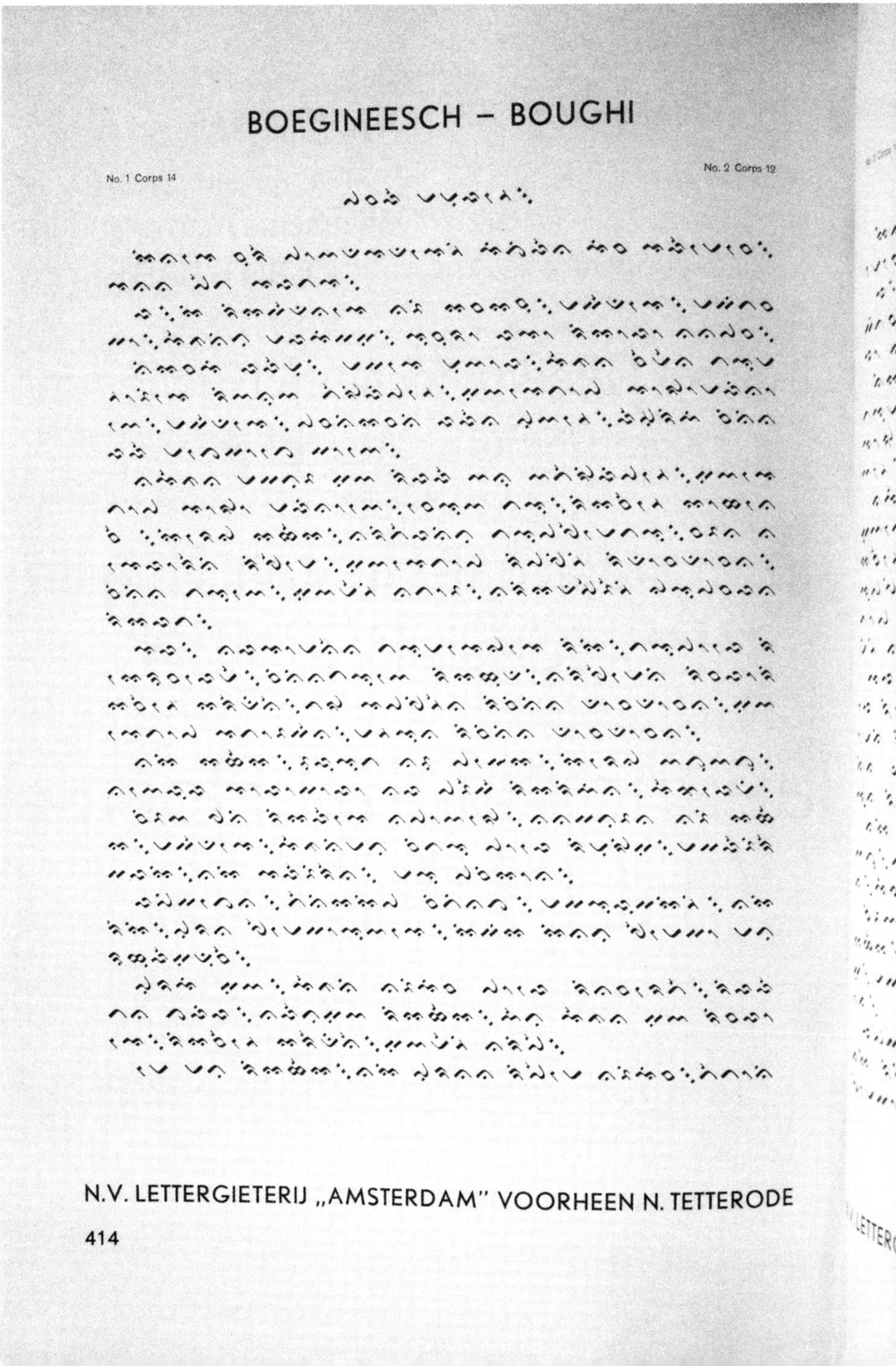

BOEGINEESCH – BOUGHI

No. 1 Corps 14

No. 2 Corps 12

N.V. LETTERGIETERIJ „AMSTERDAM" VOORHEEN N. TETTERODE

414

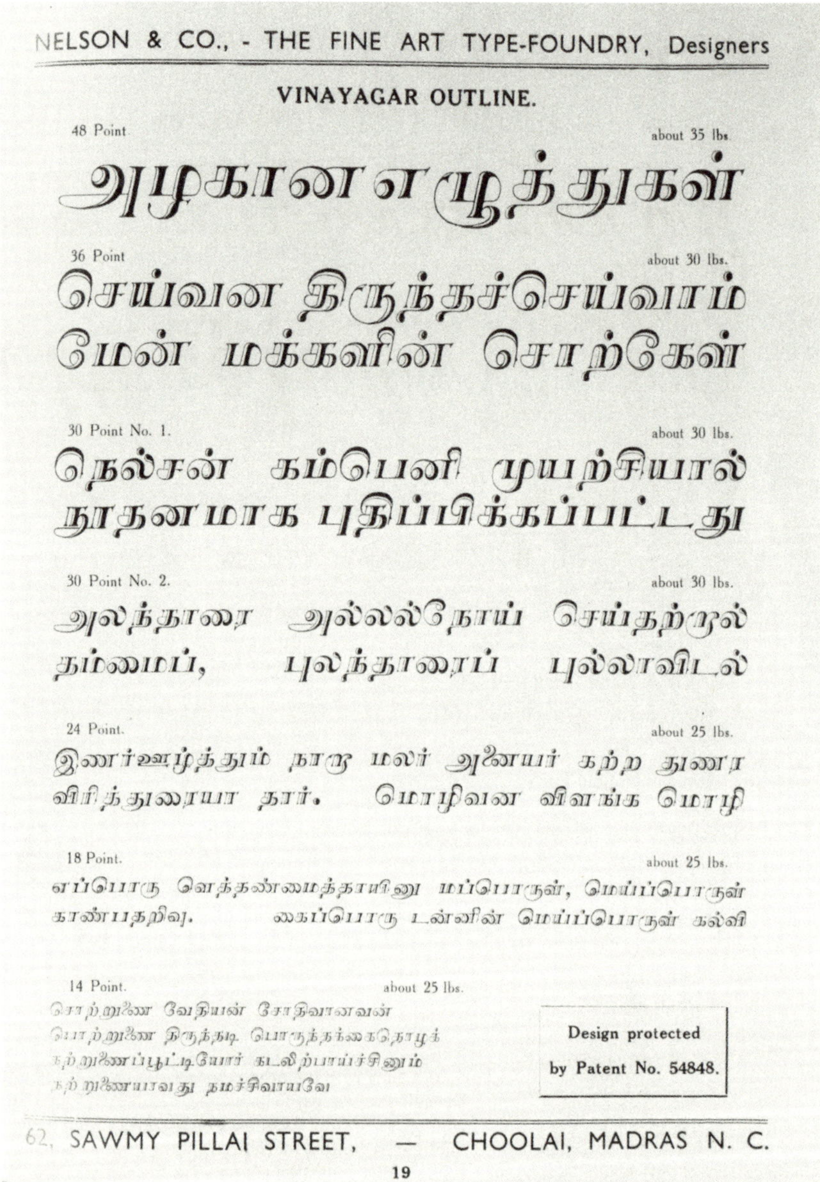

NELSON & CO., - THE FINE ART TYPE-FOUNDRY, Designers

VINAYAGAR OUTLINE.

48 Point about 35 lbs.

அழகான எழுத்துகள்

36 Point about 30 lbs.

செய்வன திருந்தச்செய்வாம்
மேன் மக்களின் சொற்கேள்

30 Point No. 1. about 30 lbs.

நெல்சன் கம்பெனி முயற்சியால்
நூதனமாக பதிப்பிக்கப்பட்டது

30 Point No. 2. about 30 lbs.

அலந்தாரை அல்லல்நோய் செய்தற்றால்
தம்மைப், புலந்தாரைப் புல்லாவிடல்

24 Point. about 25 lbs.

இணர்ஊழ்த்தும் நாறு மலர் அனையர் கற்ற துணர
விரித்துரையா தார். மொழிவன விளங்க மொழி

18 Point. about 25 lbs.

எப்பொரு ளெத்தன்மைத்தாயினு மப்பொருள், மெய்ப்பொருள்
காண்பதறிவு. கைப்பொரு டன்னின் மெய்ப்பொருள் கல்வி

14 Point. about 25 lbs.

சொற்றுணை வேதியன் சோதிவானவன்
பொற்றுணை திருந்தடி பொருந்தக்கைதொழக்
கற்றுணைப்பூட்டியோர் கடலிற்பாய்ச்சினும்
நற்றுணையாவது நமச்சிவாயவே

Design protected
by Patent No. 54848.

62, SAWMY PILLAI STREET, — CHOOLAI, MADRAS N. C.

19

SB 12 *Specimen of Tamil types designed by Mr A. K. Manicka Mudaliar,* Madras: Nelson & Co, *c* 1938. 290 × 255 mm.

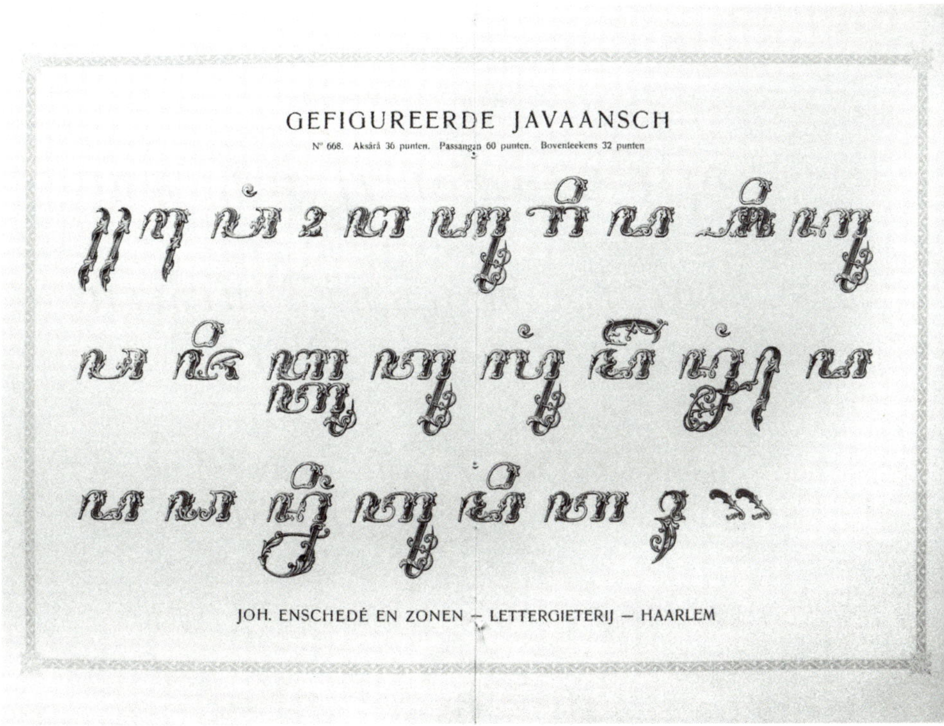

SB **13** Javanese types in *Oostersche schriften*, Haarlem: Joh. Enschedé en Zonen, *c* 1913. 297 × 420 mm (double-page).

SB **14** Galley with the original non-Latin typesetting of the Bengali and Modi type specimen, handset by Fiona Ross with types cast by Oxford University Press from early nineteenth-century matrices from the Charles Wilkins typographic collection now held at the British Library. London: St Bride Printing Library, 1981. ➤

SB **15** Specimen of Bengali and Modi types, set by Fiona Ross at St Bride Library (later published in *Matrix* 7, Winter, 1987). 265 × 190 mm. ➤

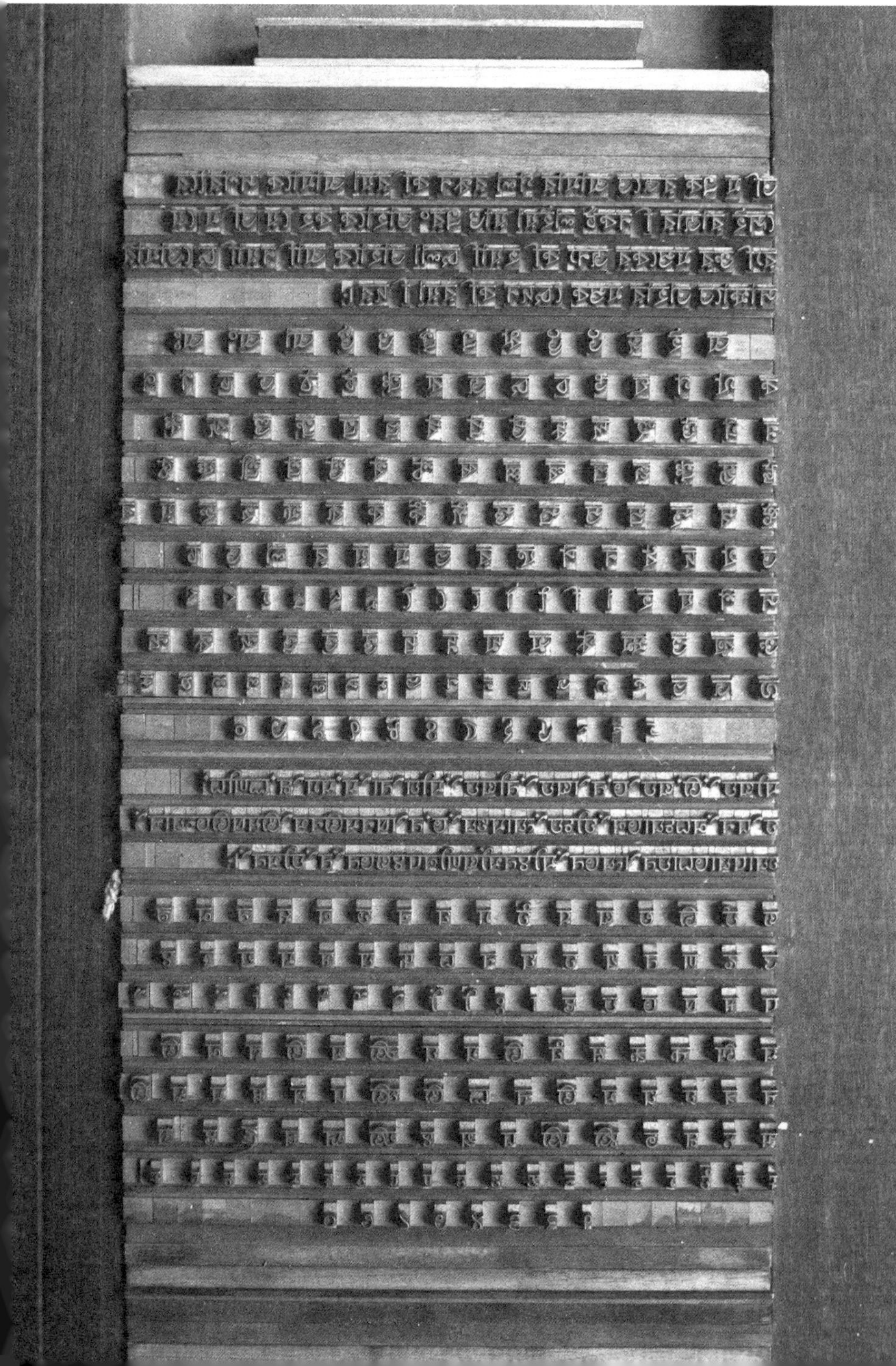

The Bengali and Modi Types

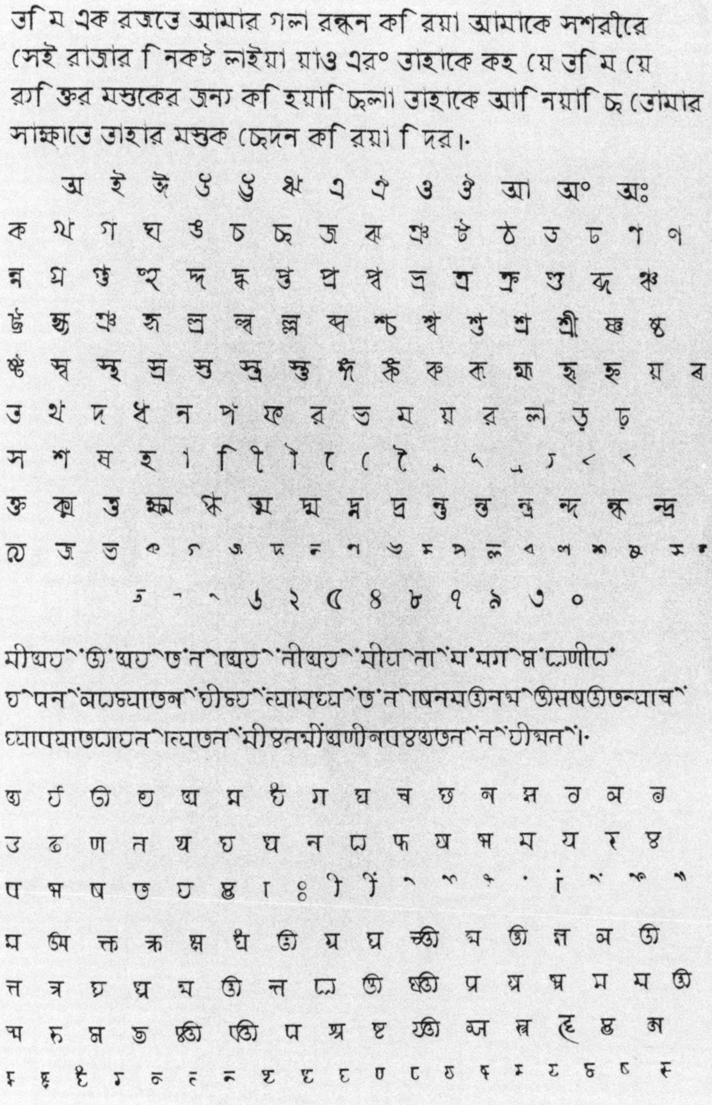

'MONOTYPE' BURMESE LIGHT

SERIES No. 558

18 POINT | 12¾ SET

၁၈၉၇ ခုနှစ်တွင် အင်္ဂလန်ပြည်သို့ ခေတ်မှီ တိုးတက်လာသော စက်တစက် ရောက်ရှိလာလေသည်။ ၎င်းစက်ကို ဦးစွာ အမေရိကန်လူမျိုး စတင်တည်ထွင်သူ တဦးဖြစ်သော တောလဘတ်လင်(န)စတန် က ခဲလက်ချောင်းများမှ ခဲစာလုံး မျက်နှာပြင်များ သီးခြားထွက်ရှိလာလေအောင် လေပေါက်စက္ကူလိပ်ဖြင့် ဖန်တီး၍ ရုပ်လုံးကိုဖေါ်ခဲ့လေသည်။ နောက်များမကြာမီ လင်(န)စတန်နှင့် ဂျွန်စဲလားဘင်ဂရောက်(ဖ)ဆိုသူ အင်ဂျင်နီယာကြီးတို့သည် စာလုံးများအား တိုင်းထွာချိန်ဆနိုင်သော စာစီ နှင့် စာလုံးသွင်းစက်တစက်ကို ထပ်မံ တဆင့်တက်၍ ပြုလုပ်လိုက်ကြလေသည်။ ဤသို့ ပြုလုပ်လိုက်သောစက်သည် နောက်များမကြာမီပင် ခေတ်မှီ "မိုနိုတိုက်" စက်များ ဟူ၍ ခေါ်ဝေါ် ပြောင်းလဲလာလေသည်။

ဤစက်ကို ၁၈၉၇ခုနှစ်က အင်္ဂလန်သို့ တင်ပို့စဉ်ဝယ် အဓိက ရည်ရွယ်ချက်မှာ လူအများ ကြည့်ရှုရန် ပြသခြင်းသာ ဖြစ်ပေသေးသည်။ ဤစက်ကို ထပ်မံ ဖြည့်စွက် တပ်ဆင်လိုက်သည့် လေနှင့်သွားလာ ပြုလုပ်နိုင်သော စာစီ လက်နှိပ်စက်ခုံနှင့် အက္ခရာ ပြည့်စုံစွာရှိသော စာလုံးပုံစံ အိမ်ခွက် (မက်ထရစ်) တို့အပါအဝင် အဆင်သင့်ဖြစ်ပြီး ရောင်းချနိုင်ခဲ့သည်မှာ၊ ၁၈၉၉ခုနှစ်သို့ မတိုင်မခြင်း မဖြစ်မြောက်ခဲ့ပေ၊ ၎င်းနှစ် ၁၈၉၉ခုနှစ်၌ ဆားရေးနယ်၊ရက်(ဒ)ဟီးမြို့တွင် စက်ရုံ လုပ်ငန်းကြီးကို စတင် တည်ထောင်လိုက်လေသည်။

ယင်းသို့သော အခါသမယက ဆိုလျှင် မည်သူတဦးတယောက်မျှ အသစ် ရောက်ရှိလာသော စက်မှာ စာစီခန်းဌာနအဘို့ ရိုးရိုး ခဲစာလုံး စက်ရုံများမှ ပြုလုပ်လိုက်သော အကောင်းဆုံး စာလုံး များကို စာလုံးခွက်ထဲ၌ထည့်၍ လက်ဖြင့် စီသွားသောစာများနှင့် နှိုင်းယှဉ်ရာတွင် လှပ၍ အရေးပါ ခရီးရောက်နိုင်မည့်အကြောင်းကို မှန်းဆတွေးတောဝံ့နိုင်အံ့မည်နည်း။ သို့သော် ဒုတိယ ရာစုသို့ ပြောင်းလဲလာလေရာ၊ နှစ်ဆယ် ရာစုသို့ ရောက်ခဲ့သည်မူ၊ ကောင်းမွန်ခြင်းအကြောင်းအရပ်ရပ်များ ပွင့်လင်း ပေါ်ပေါက်လာလေသည်။

၁၉၁၈ခုနှစ် ကျော်လွန်၍ နှစ်များ များမကြာမီပင် "မိုနိုတိုက်" စက်များနှင့် လိုအပ်သည့် တန်းဆာပလာ ပစ္စည်း အမျိုးမျိုးတို့ကို အင်္ဂလန်ပြည်တွင် ပြုလုပ်ဆောင်ရွက်လာခဲ့လေသည်။ အထူးတလည် စူးစိုက်၍ စာလုံးများ ပုံသွင်းခြင်း၊ ပြုလုပ်ခြင်းများကို ဆောင်ရွက်ခဲ့ရာတွင်၊ ပုံနှိပ် ရာဇဝင်တွင် မည်သည့်ကုမ္ပဏီ တဦးတလေမျှ မပြုလုပ်ခဲ့ကြသေးသော လုပ်ငန်းကို ပြုလုပ်လိုက် လေသည်။ မကြာမီပင် ပုံနှိပ်လုပ်ငန်းများမှ အသိအမှတ် အလေးပြုခြင်းကို ခံယူရရှိလာပေသည်။

5-55

PRINTED IN GREAT BRITAIN BY THE MONOTYPE CORPORATION LIMITED AT THEIR WORKS, SALFORDS, REDHILL, SURREY, ENGLAND. REGISTERED ADDRESS: MONOTYPE HOUSE, 43 FETTER LANE, LONDON, E.C.4

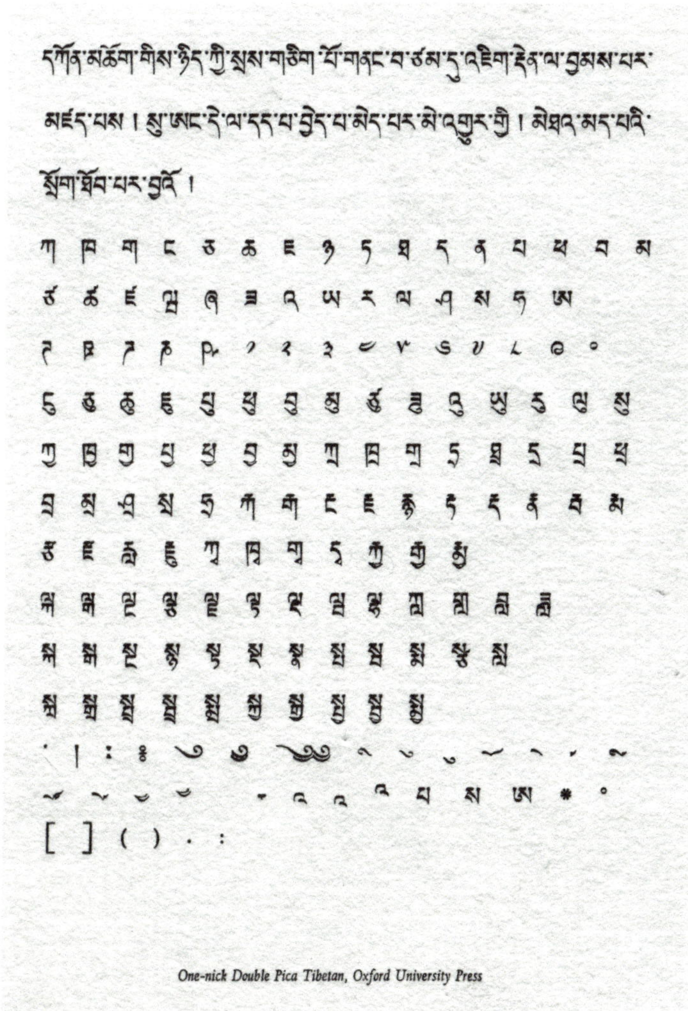

SB 17 Specimen of Tibetan types handset by Jo De Baerdemaeker at St Bride Library, Oxford: Alembic Press, 2007. 240 × 165 mm.

SB 16 Monotype Burmese Light, Series no. 558, London: Monotype Corporation, 1953. 270 × 222 mm.

The Linotype Non-Latin Collection, University of Reading

Fiona Ross specializes in non-Latin type design and typography. From 1978 to 1989 she worked for Linotype Ltd (UK) and was responsible for the design of Linotype's non-Latin fonts and typesetting schemes. Since 1989 she has worked as a consultant, type designer and visiting lecturer, and in 2003 joined the Department of Typography & Graphic Communication at the University Reading as a part-time lecturer.

The Linotype Non-Latin Collection forms part of the Type Drawing and Specimen Collection housed in the Department of Typography & Graphic Communication at the University of Reading. It comprises artwork and accompanying material of non-Latin fonts developed by Linotype & Machinery Ltd and by the Department of Typographic Development at the associated firm of Linotype Ltd (originally Linotype-Paul) during the course of the twentieth-century until the latter's closure in 1996. This collection's artefacts testify to this period being of particular significance for it witnessed extensive changes in typemaking and typesetting technologies and in the type-manufacturing industry.

The holding consists of original artwork and supporting material for a wide range of languages or writing-systems, namely Arabic and related scripts: Farsi, Jawi, Kurdish, Pushtu, Sindhi, Urdu; the North Indian scripts: Assamese, Bengali, Devanagari, Gujarati, Gurmukhi, Oriya; the South Indian scripts: Kannada, Malayalam, Tamil, Telugu, and also Sinhala. Other scripts include Amharic (Ethiopic), Burmese, Greek, Hebrew, and Thai, with supplementary material on Cyrillic and a few scripts, such as Lao, that were not developed into fonts by Linotype Ltd. The Collection also holds drawings for Tracy's Times Europa typeface as well as Karnak Black.

The bulk of the artwork in the Collection was produced by the British Linotype letter-drawing studio, originally under the direction of Walter Tracy, who had established the Department

Photograph of a shipment of Model 6 Linotype machines leaving the Linotype & Machinery Works, Altrincham, Cheshire en route to the Bengal Secretariat Press, Calcutta, *Linotype Record*, January, 1923.

of Typographic Development in 1974, and then myself from 1979. The Collection also contains designs by former Linotype employees who continued as consultant designers, notably Matthew Carter and Tim Holloway, as well as artwork by commissioned designers such as Georges Dib. Walter Tracy, who had joined Linotype & Machinery Ltd in 1948, continued to act as Linotype's design consultant after his retirement.

The Linotype Non-Latin Collection holds thousands of original letter-drawings that have been preserved in their original hanging folders. The medium used was either pencil on paper or ink on drafting film. The scale of these drawings also varies according to the technology for which they were produced, or even according to the preferences of the designer. The customary drawings during Tracy's time at the Department comprised pencil drawings of approximately 12 inches on paper. From these, hand-cut negatives [friskets] would be made from rubilith film (see RU 3) which would be sent either to Linotype

Walter Tracy, 1914–1995.

Mergenthaler Co in America or to D Stempel AG in Germany for font manufacture.

The drawings and friskets were register-punched and aligned with a transparent background drawing-mask by means of a pin-bar in order to ensure perfect character fit – a particularly essential requirement for joining scripts. Each typestyle would have its own drawing-mask produced by the Department showing the baseline, the kerning area and the size of the typesetting window along with vertical lines spaced according to the relative unit-width system employed (see RU **16** and RU **31**). Earlier typefaces would have different drawing-masks for the different master sizes, many of which are preserved in the Collection, and would have used the relative-unit system of 18 units to the em for determining character widths. In the 1970s the more refined system of 54 units to the em was adopted until the even more flexible system of 1000 units was available in PostScript font production in the late 1980s. The artwork in the Collection bears witness to such transitions and provides visible evidence of other technological changes, often conveyed by the notes on the drawings that denote, for example, vertical or horizontal shifts to cater for deep Urdu typeforms (see RU **33**) or particularly wide Telugu ligatures (see RU **14**).

Inked drawings generally represent the development of photographic, rather than hand-cut, friskets being made; this became standard practice from 1987. A single drawing would be used for several characters if the basic letterform was the same (see RU **6** and RU **21**), not simply as a labour-saving device but to ensure image constancy. Sketches and 'roughs' have been preserved of many of Linotype's non-Latin digital typefaces showing experimentation in design (see RU **2** and RU **32**) and design revisions (see RU **11** and RU **13**) that deliberately exploited new developments in digitization. Photographic trials (see RU **18**) and printed test samples of numerous letterforms have been retained with the finished artwork. Unfortunately, until the 1980s it was customary for the drawings to indicate only, by initials, the person who had checked the drawings rather than show the identity of the letter-drawer.

The Department of Typographic Development, situated in Cheltenham during the 1980s and early 1990s, was particularly active in the design and development of original non-Latin digital fonts, particularly Indian, alongside the customary activity of developing and/or adapting existing or commissioned designs (mainly Arabic) for the new technologies. A strong team of designers and researchers, many of whom stayed for well over a decade including the letter-drawing studio supervisor Georgina Surman, ensured continuity in the design of large in-house projects, such as a new Sinhala typeface for Sri Lankan publications.

The Department, which was also responsible for the design of keyboard layouts, typesetting schemes, software specifications, font encodings, screen fonts for proofing (RU **23**), accent positioning, and post-production testing, benefited from the support of a dedicated non-Latin software team initially headed by Dr Mike Fellows. It was the continuing close relationship of the Typographic Department with Linotype's software developers initiated by Tracy that enabled Linotype to develop pioneering keyboarding techniques and typography for Arabic photocomposition, and which in 1978 led to the invention of the Phonetic Keyboard for Indian scripts by Dr Mike Fellows and myself, and the patented invention of Nasta'liq typesetting with the Sheeraz typeface in 1987. Such innovations, which transformed keyboarding practices for complex scripts, and concomitantly the design process and consequent typography, are well documented in the Linotype archive. The team of software programmers also supported the undertaking of non-Latin PostScript font manufacture by the Department from 1988.

Further support, especially related to linguistic issues, came from the associated company of Linotype India Associates Private Ltd based in Bombay (Mumbai) and the Linotype Middle East Liaison Office located in Beirut and later in Nicosia, as well as from good relationships with Linotype agents in countries such as Pakistan and Thailand. Documents showing the development of projects and the exchange of ideas with colleagues across the world, including those at Mergenthaler Linotype and Stempel, are held in the research and development files from Linotype Ltd and have been preserved with the Collection. Correspondence with prominent newspaper proprietors and other customers with specific requirements are also preserved. Research conducted at the School of Oriental and African Studies (University of London), the British Library, and particularly at the St Bride Library underpinned the non-Latin type development work, as is attested by the supplementary notes to be found in the archive. All this material in the Collection provides vital information about design decisions, technological developments and linguistic requirements that are reflected in the finished Linotype non-Latin fonts.

Following the closure of Linotype Ltd (latterly named Linotype-Hell Ltd), the font data, the letter-drawings and accompanying material produced by the Department of Typographic Development were transported to Linotype GmbH (then Linotype Library) in Germany in 1997. After spending several years housed in a cellar at the company's office in Bad Homburg, the archive was generously donated by Linotype GmbH to the Department of Typography & Graphic Communication at the University of Reading.

The Department of Typographic Development, letter-drawing studio and research staff, 1983 (left to right: Georgina Surman, Lesley Sewell, Sarah Morley, Gillian Robertson, Ros Coates, Fiona Ross, and Donna Yandle).

Although not all the original materials could be preserved, the Collection is a unique resource: it offers exceptional insight into the development of typographic resources for the non-Latin world. Especially in its coverage of Arabic/Perso-Arabic and Indian scripts (that includes 31 Arabic and 26 Indian digital fonts), the Collection captures original and otherwise rare documents of the typemaking process. In societies where the range of typographic choices has been, mostly for engineering reasons, much narrower than for Latin script users, the typefaces represented in the Collection reflect an overwhelming proportion of the experience of local readers. For example, the typefaces documented in the Collection for Arabic, which include the renowned Yakout, Lotus and Qadi fonts, represent 95 per cent of the Arabic-script newspaper output in the period, and 80 per cent of the remaining commercial printing. In India, Linotype had 90 per cent of the vernacular newspaper market by the late 1980s, and its original typeface designs remain in popular use.

Today the Linotype Non-Latin Collection provides a valuable research and teaching resource. A selection of items from the Collection recently exhibited at the University of Reading are shown in the following pages; spanning almost a century, they provide a glimpse into the type-design and font manufacturing processes that track typographic developments across technologies and time in a variety of writing systems.

Fiona Ross, 'An approach to non-Latin type design', *Language Culture Type*, New York: Association Typographique International (ATypI), 2002. pp 65–75.

— 'Non-Latin Type Design at Linotype' *http://stbride.org/friends/conference/twentiethcenturygraphiccommunication/NonLatin.html*

— 'A design for Sri Lanka', *Building Letters Three (tsunami edition)*, Prague, 2006. pp 20–3.

Walter Tracy, 'Advances in Arabic Printing', *Bulletin (British Society for Middle Eastern Studies)*, vol. 2, no. 2, Taylor & Francis Ltd, 1975. pp 87–93.

— *Letters of Credit*, Bedford: Gordon Fraser Gallery, 1986.

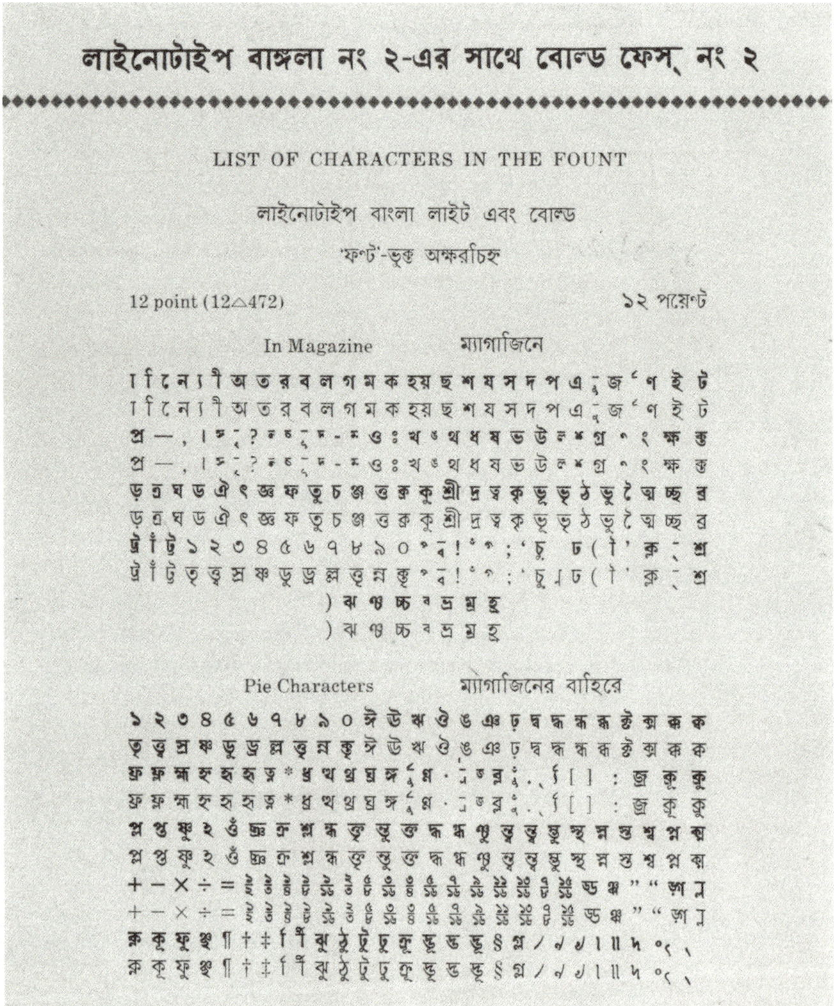

লাইনোটাইপ বাঙ্গলা নং ২-এর সাথে বোল্ড ফেস্ নং ২

LIST OF CHARACTERS IN THE FOUNT

লাইনোটাইপ বাংলা লাইট এবং বোল্ড

'ফণ্ট'-ভুক্ত অক্ষরচিহ্ন

12 point (12△472) ১২ পয়েণ্ট

In Magazine ম্যাগাজিনে

Pie Characters ম্যাগাজিনের বাহিরে

RU 1 Hot-metal fount synopsis: Linotype Bengali, *c* 1968–9.

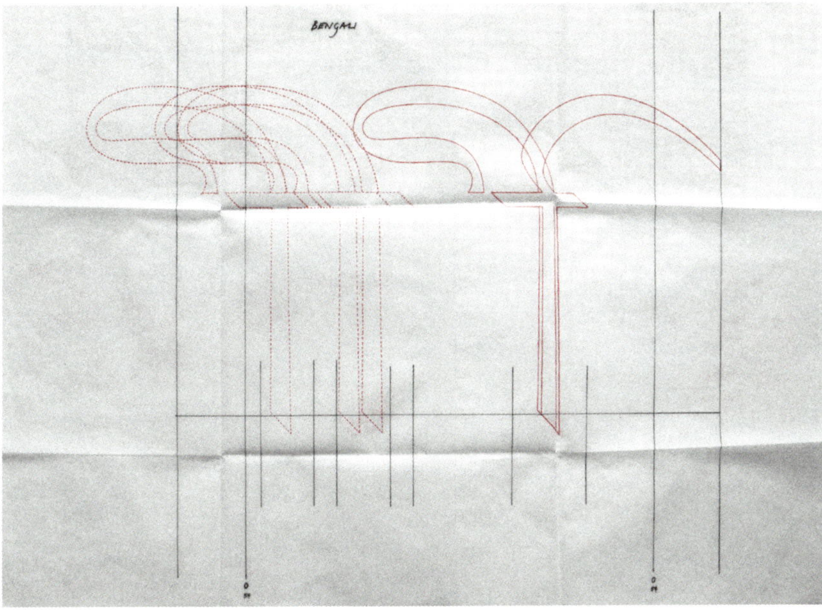

RU 2 Drawing templates for kerning vowel signs utilizing available offsets for digital type in Bengali by Tim Holloway, *c* 1978.

RU 3 Scan from a hand-cut rubylith frisket of Linotype Bengali character 'Srì'.

RU 4 Linotype Devanagari drawing of typeform 'chva' for filmsetting, by Matthew Carter, *c* 1975.

RU 5 Linotype Devanagari drawing revision of typeform 'chva' for digital fonts by Linotype letter-drawing studio, *c* 1983.

RU6 Rohini Bold letter-drawing of three Devanagari typeforms, 1986 and 1988.

તા. ૧૫-૮-૮૫

છેલ્લા વર્ષોમાં નબળા વર્ગને બેઠા કરવાના
૨૦ મુદ્દી કાર્યક્રમો નીચે હાંસલ કરેલી
પ્રગતિમાં દેશે મોખરાનું સ્થાન મેળવ્યું છે
—મુખ્ય મંત્રી

RU 7 Section of a flong for a Gujarati newspaper using Linotype Gujarati, 1985.

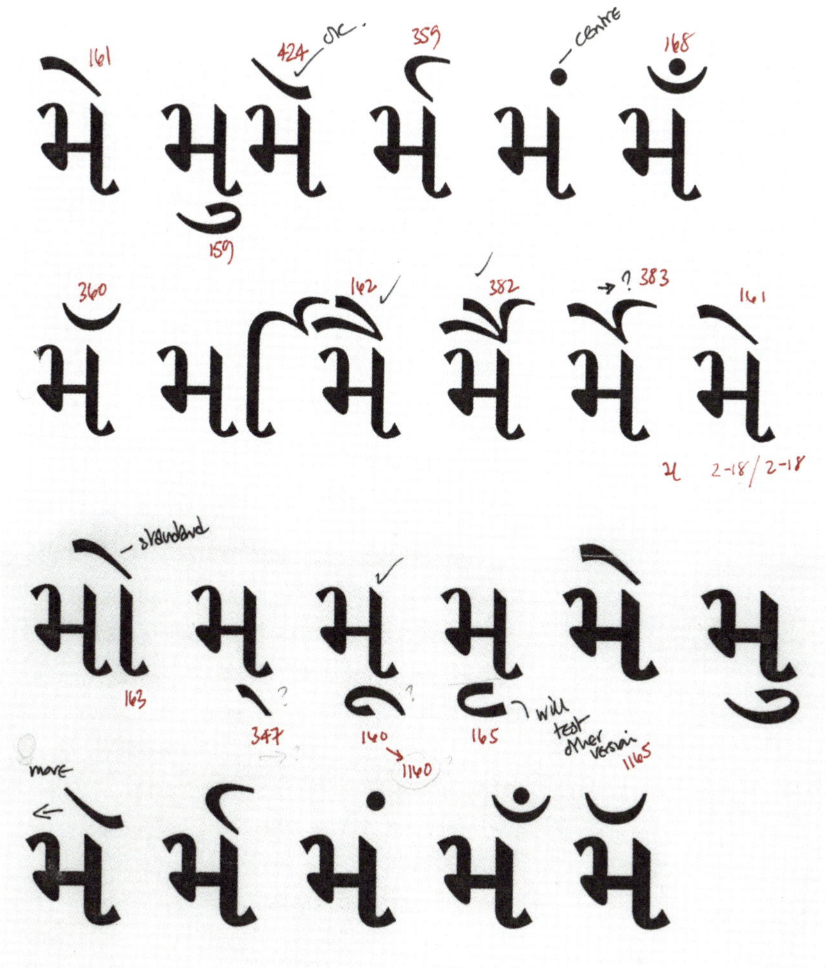

RU8 Accent placement test of Linotype Gujarati Bold, PostScript fonts, 1989.

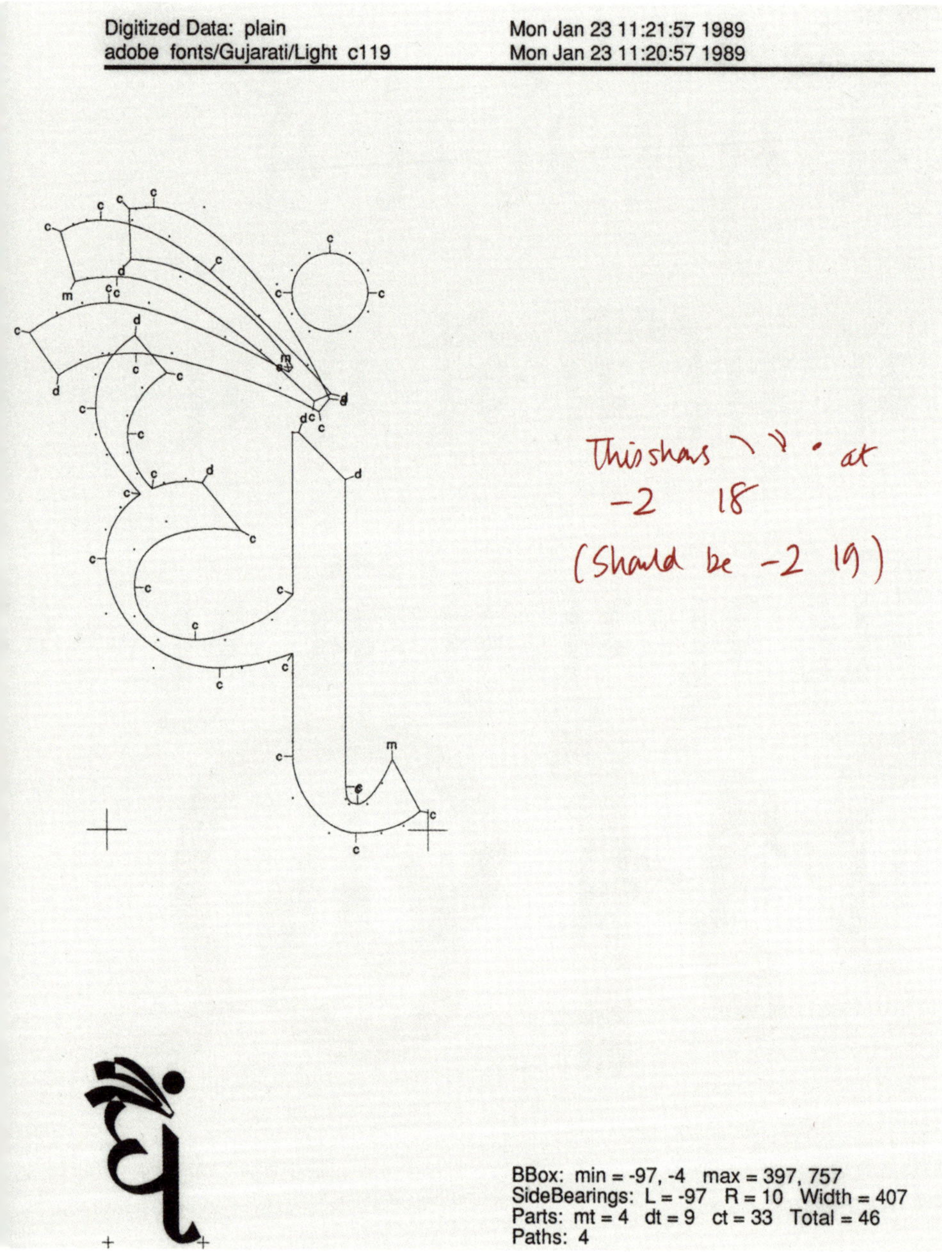

RU9 Gujarati PostScript 'digiplot' showing 'accent' positioning, 1989.

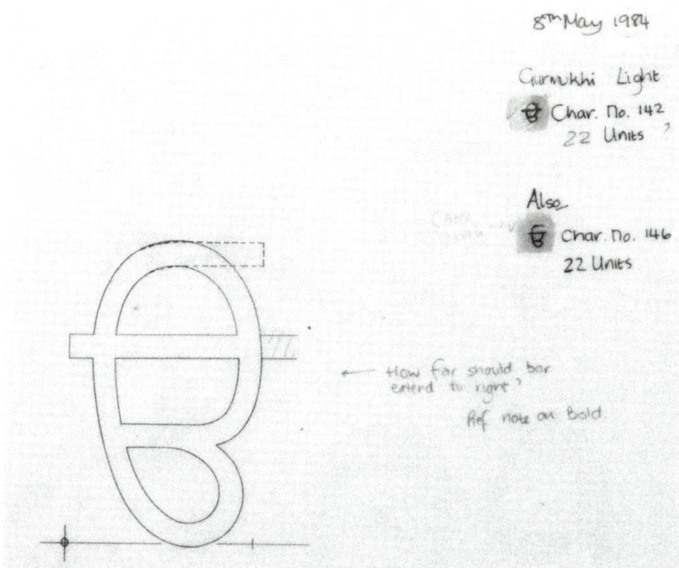

RU **10** Linotype Gurmukhi Light letter-drawing for digital fonts, 1984.

RU **11** Linotype Gurmukhi Bold 'rough' sketch, showing correction, as preparation for digital designs, 1984.

RU **12** Linotype Oriya Bold finished artwork for digital fonts, 1984.

Revision
Revised shape
56 units

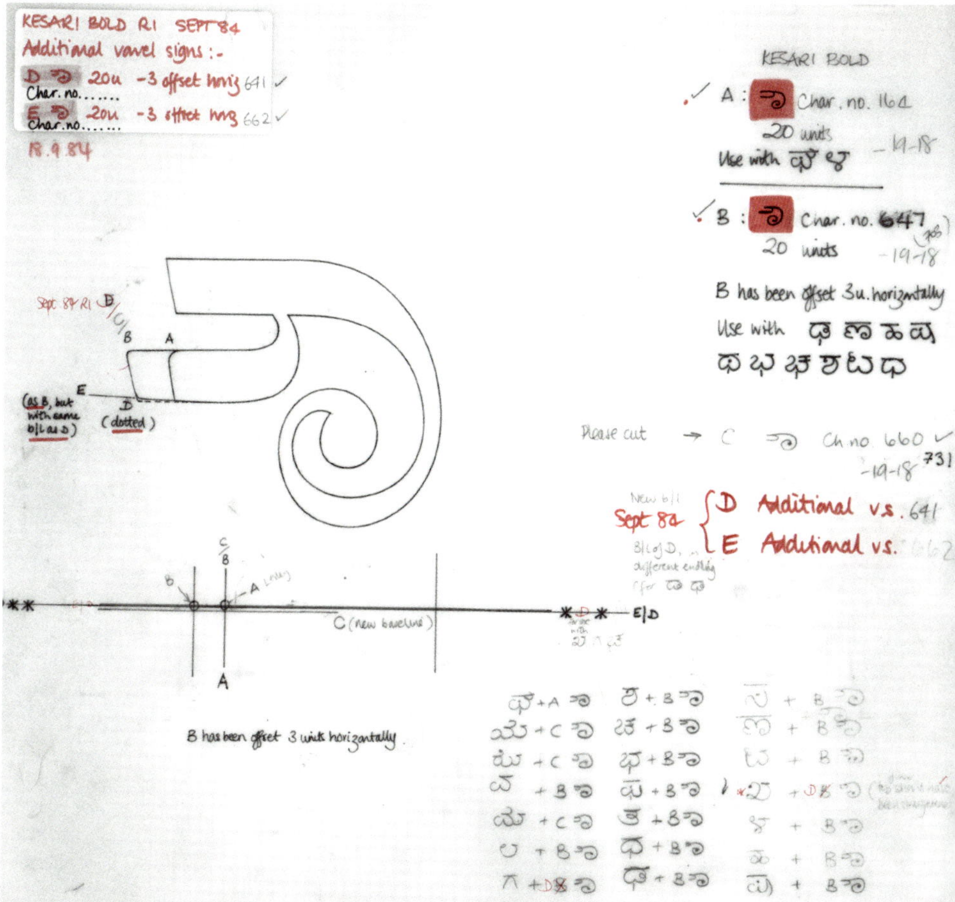

RU 15 Kesari Bold vowel sign for Kannada ligatures for digital fonts, 1983 and 1984.

RU 13 Rough and finished artwork for revised Kannada digital typeform, 1986.

RU 14 Telugu Bold (later named Tamara) drawing of wide character with horizontal offset for digitization.

RU 16 Telugu Light artwork on drawing-mask.

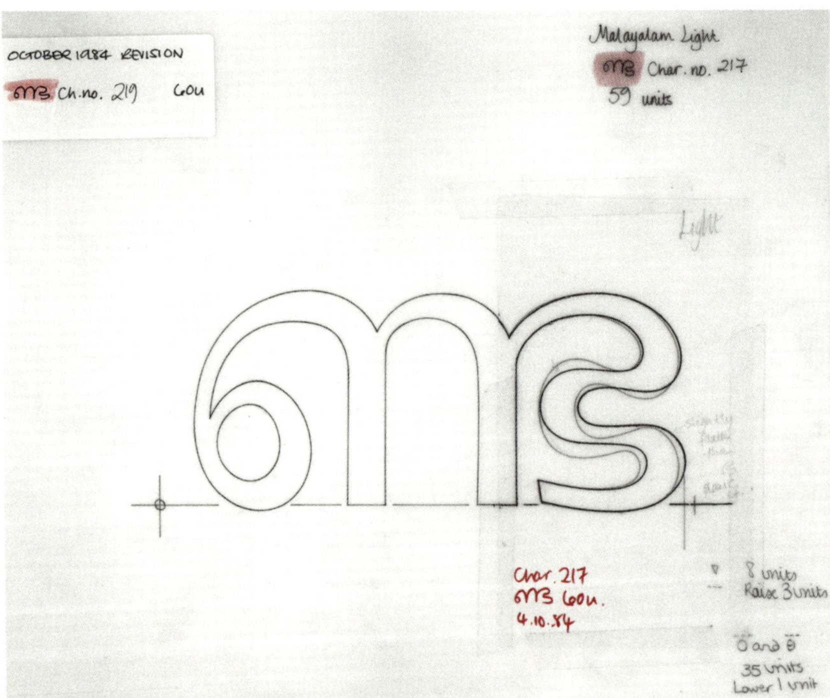

RU 17 Malayalam Light (later named Manorama) drawing with revision, 1984.

RU 18 Photographic reduction and paste-up of artwork for Malayalam digital fonts.

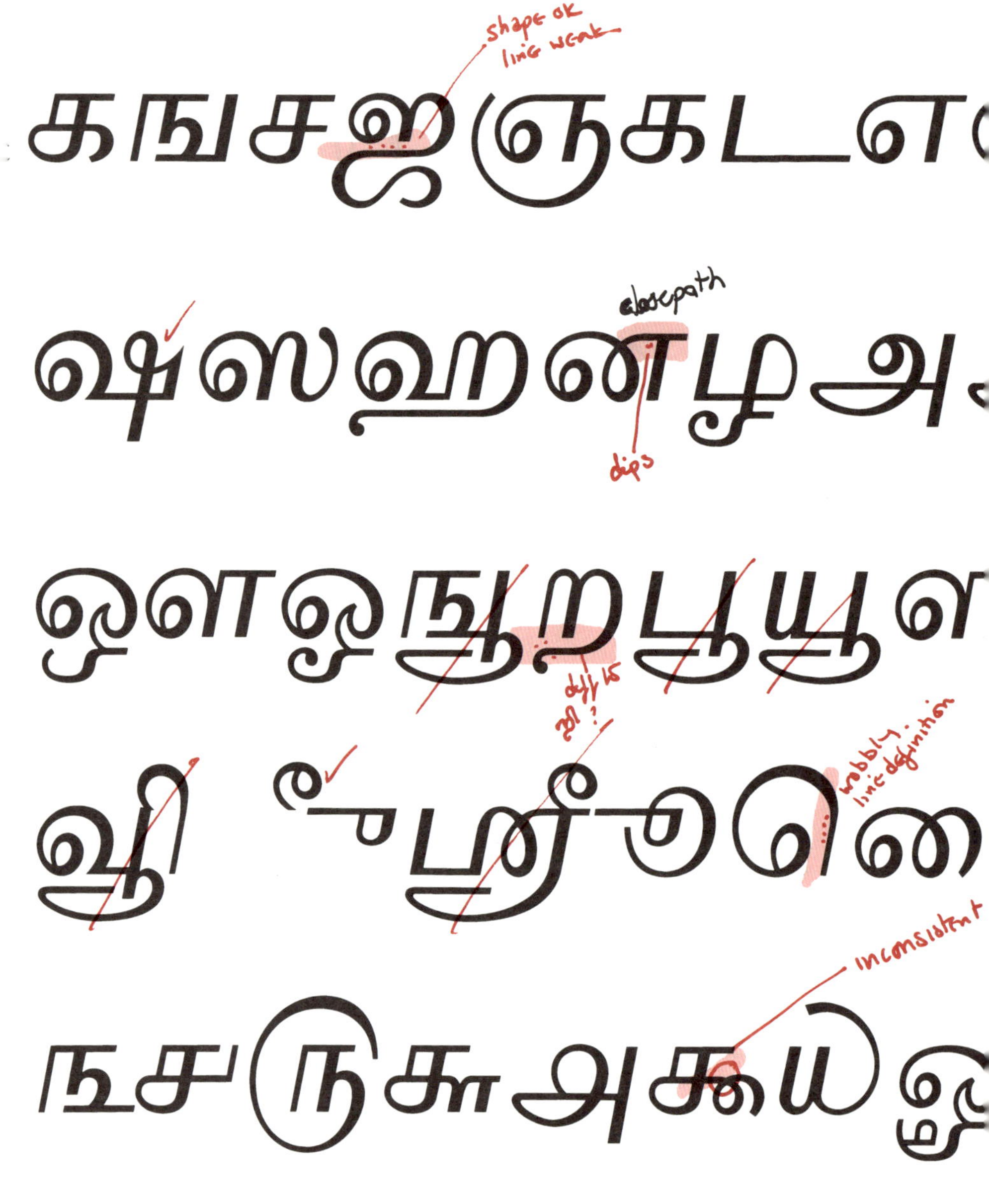

RU 19 Tamil script: Samanti Light PostScript output critiqued by Fiona Ross, 1993.

RU 21 Sinhala Bold artwork for two characters from photographic copy of finished artwork.

RU 22 Sinhala (later named Araliya) Light standard preliminary sidebearing test between 'H' from Linotronic 202 font, 1985.

RU 23 Printed tests of Araliya screen fonts for Apple Macintosh PostScript fonts, 1992.

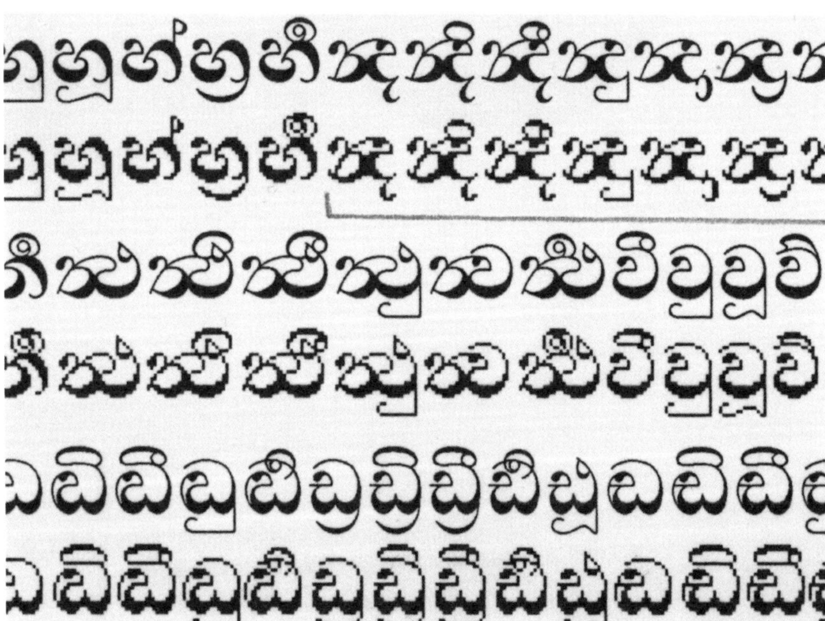

****
* ບົດ ຄວາມ *
****

ຂໍ້ຜູກມັດ ຂອງ ວຽດນາມເໜືອ ກັບ ແນວລາວ

ເມື່ອວັນທີ ໑໐ ພຶສພາ ໑໙໗໑ ທີ່ຜ່ານມານີ້ ຜູ້ນຳແນວລາວຮັກຊາດ ຈຳນວນໜຶ່ງ ໄດ້ເຊັນສັນຍາຜູກມັດຕ່າງໆ ທີ່ພວກເພິ່ນເອີ້ນວ່າ "ຖແລງການຮ່ວມ" ກັບຜູ້ນຳຮາໂນຍ ເພື່ອຈັກຈູງເອົາລາວທັງຊາດເປັນຂີ້ຂ້ອຍຂ້າແກວເໜືອ ຢ່າງສົມບູນແບບຕໍ່ໄປ ຄຳສັນຍາຜູກມັດຕ່າງໆນັ້ນ ຂຶ້ນຕົ້ນດ້ວຍການກ່າວວ່າ ດຳເນີນໄປດ້ວຍສັນຖວະໄມຕຣີແບບສູ້ຮົບ ຊຶ່ງເຮົາແປໄດ້ຄວາມວ່າ ວຽດນາມເໜືອ ຈະຕ້ອງອາໃສຜູ້ນຳແນວລາວຮັກຊາດ ເປັນເຄື່ອງບັງໜ້າຮຸກຮານ ພຣະຣາຊອານາຈັກລາວ ແລະ ຂ້າຄົນລາວຕໍ່ໄປຢ່າງບໍ່ສິ້ນສຸດ ແລ້ວຜູ້ນຳແນວລາວຮັກຊາດ ຍັງໃຫ້ສັນຍາກັບພວກເຂົາວ່າ ຈະເອົາຊື່ປະຊາຊົນອອກບັງໜ້າ ອວດອ້າງວ່າເປັນການຕໍ່ສູ້ຂອງປະຊາຊົນ ແລະ ປະຊາຊົນກໍຈະຕ້ອງໄດ້ຮັບໄຊຊະນະ ທີ່ແທ້ກໍໝາຍຄວາມແຕ່ພຽງວ່າ ຈະເອົາປະຊາຊົນໄປເປັນລົມໄດ ໃຕ່ໄປສູ່ໄຊຊະນະຂອງປະຕິການ ວຽດນາມເໜືອເທົ່ານັ້ນເອງ.

ຂໍ້ຜູກມັດດັ່ງກ່າວ ຍັງໄດ້ມີປະຣິຍາຍອອກໄປຢ່າງຍືດຍາວວ່າ ໃນຊີວິດເປັນຢູ່ ຂອງປະຊາຊົນໃນເຂດທີ່ວຽດນາມເໜືອຮຸກຮານແໜ້ນໜາດີຂຶ້ນ ປະຊາຊົນມ່ວນຊື່ນ ສນຸກສນານ ກ້ອນກຳລັງປະຊາຊົນສາມັກຄີຍິ່ງຂຶ້ນ ແລະສັນຕິພາບຈະໄດ້ຮັບການຟື້ນຟູດີຂຶ້ນ ປະຣິຍາຍທີ່ເພິ່ນເວົ້າໄວ້ໃນ ຂໍ້ຜູກມັດ ທີ່ເຮັດ... ໂນຍນັ້ນ ຟັງເບິ່ງແລ້ວ ເປັນຕາຢ່າງກຽດ ແລະໜ້າເບື່ອໜ່າຍ ເພາະມັນບໍ່ມີຄວາມຈິງ ທີ່ແທ້ມີຢູ່ວ່າ ປະຊາຊົນທີ່ຢູ່ໃນເຂດຮຸກຮານ ຄວບຄຸມຂອງວຽດນາມເໜືອນັ້ນ ອັດສົນຍາກແຄ້ນທີ່ສຸດ ຈົນປະຊາຊົນຈຳນວນແສນໆ ທົນຢູ່ບໍ່ໄດ້ ຕ້ອງພາກັນອົພຍົບຫລົບເຂົ້າ ມາເພິ່ງຮົ່ມເງົາຂອງຣັຖບານ ພຣະບາດສົມເດັດ ພຣະເຈົ້າມະຫາຊີວິດ ປະຊາຊົນໄດ້ຮັບທຸກທໍຣະມານ ເພາະການບີບບັງຄັບທຸກຢ່າງ ຈາກກອງທະຫານວຽດນາມເໜືອ ປະຊາຊົນ ຈະທັນໃຈສະດວກ ແລະນັ່ງລົງດ້ວຍຄວາມສະບາຍໃຈກໍທັງຍາກ ຈະເອົາເວລາ ມາມ່ວນຊື່ນສນຸກສນານ ດັ່ງທີ່ພວກເພິ່ນໄດ້ເວົ້າໄວ້ໃນສັນຍາຂໍ້ຜູກມັດ ນັ້ນຄືສິຍາກ ແລະ ສັນຕິພາບໃນເຂດຮຸກຮານ ຈະມີຂຶ້ນບໍ່ໄດ້ເລີຍ. ເມື່ອບ້ານເມືອງ ຖືກຮຸກຮານ ປະຊາຊົນຖືກບັງຄັບຂົ່ມເຫັງ ຈາກສັດຕູຕ່າງຊາດ ແລະເສຖກິດຖືກບຽດບັງເອົາໄປໃຊ້ ໃນການຮົບຢູ່ທຸກໆວັນ ມັນເປັນການເຫລືອເຊື່ອ ທີ່ຈະມາອວດອ້າງວ່າ ສັນຕິພາບກຳລັງໄດ້ຮັບການຟື້ນຟູໃຫ້ດີຂຶ້ນ.

ນອກຈາກໃນຂໍ້ ສັນຍາຜູກມັດ ຂອງວຽດນາມເໜືອ ຍັງໄດ້ຍ້ຳເຖິງແນວຮ່ວມອິນດູຈີນພວກເພິ່ນວ່າ ຈະປົກປັກຮັກສາ ສັນຕິພາບ ໃນອິນດູຈີນ ແລະບູຣະພາອາຄະເນ ແປວ່າພວກເພິ່ນຈະຕ້ອງບໍ່ລົດລະໃນການຮຸກຮານອິນດູຈີນ ແລະ ປະເທດຕ່າງໆ ໃນອາຊີອາຄະເນ ເພື່ອໃຫ້ເປັນຕາມລັດທິທາງການເມືອງຂອງເພິ່ນ ແລະເພິ່ນຈະໄດ້ເປັນຫົວໂຈກໝູ່ໃນແຖບນີ້ ເຈຕະນາຂອງວຽດນາມເໜືອ ດັ່ງກ່າວນີ້

RU 24 Lao sample text, date unknown.

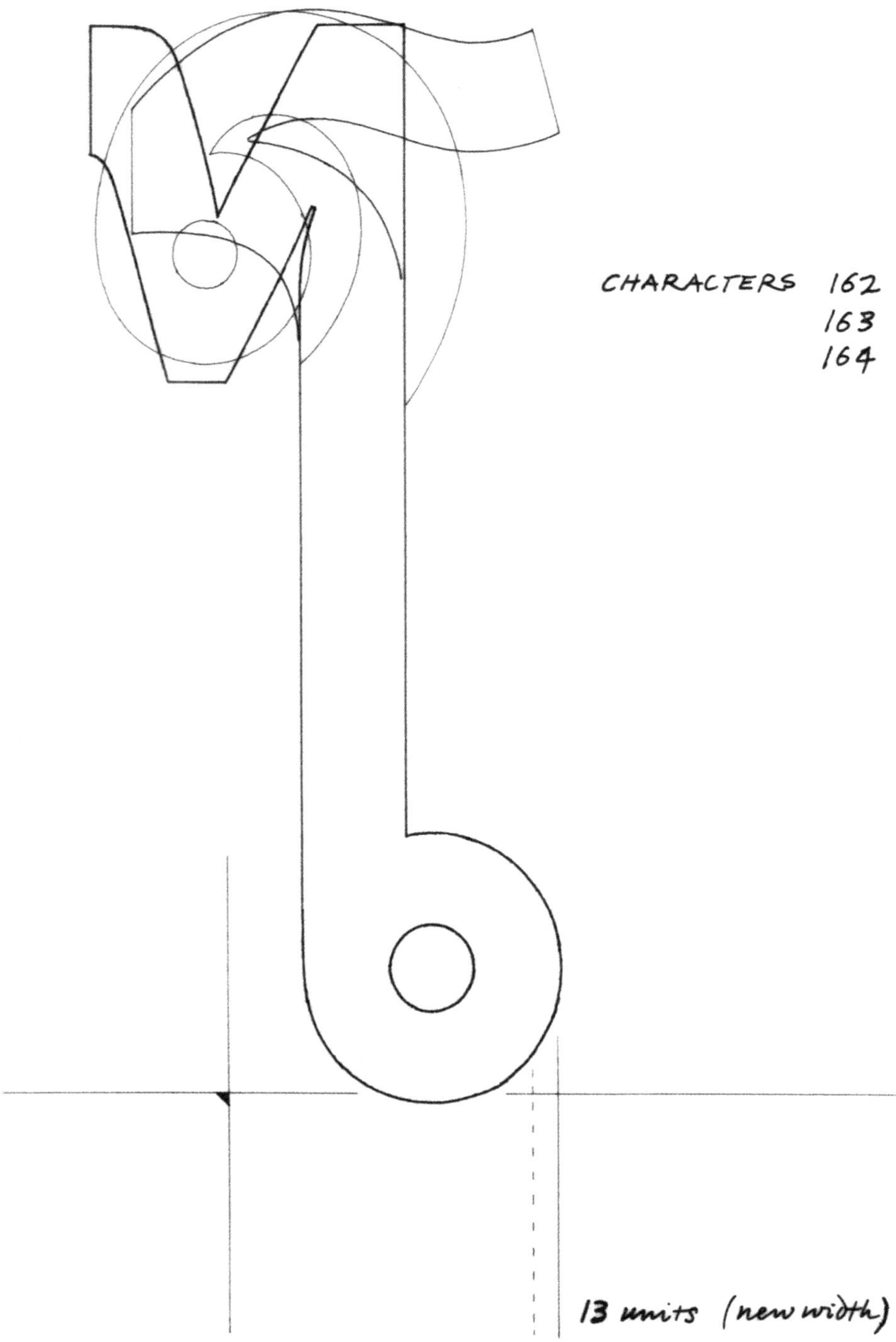
CHARACTERS 162
163
164
13 units (new width)

5. WIDTH OF CHARACTERS

The 'width' of a character includes both the width of the image itself and the appropriate space on either side of the character. A width must be defined in a number of whole units, as drawn on the mask.
The two vertical lines which show the width of a character are called the 'left side bearing' and the 'right side bearing'. (Diagram 3)

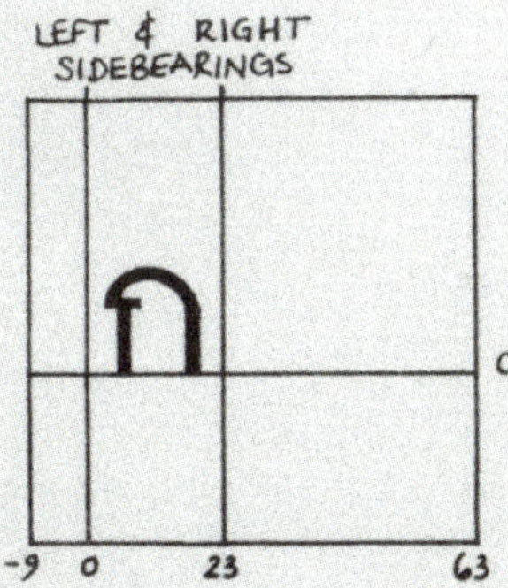

Diagram 3

6. STROKE WIDTH OF CHARACTERS

Minimum stroke widths have to be observed in order to prevent the character shape from breaking up when digitized. The minimum stroke width for a positive image is 5mm, and for a negative image 7.5mm. (Diagram 4)

Diagram 4

RU 26 Extract from Linotype in-house document 'Guidelines for the production of artwork for digital systems' for the Thai script by Fiona Ross, 1985.

RU 25 Thai Monoline (later named Sirichana) Bold letter-drawings for digital fonts by Tim Holloway, *c* 1985.

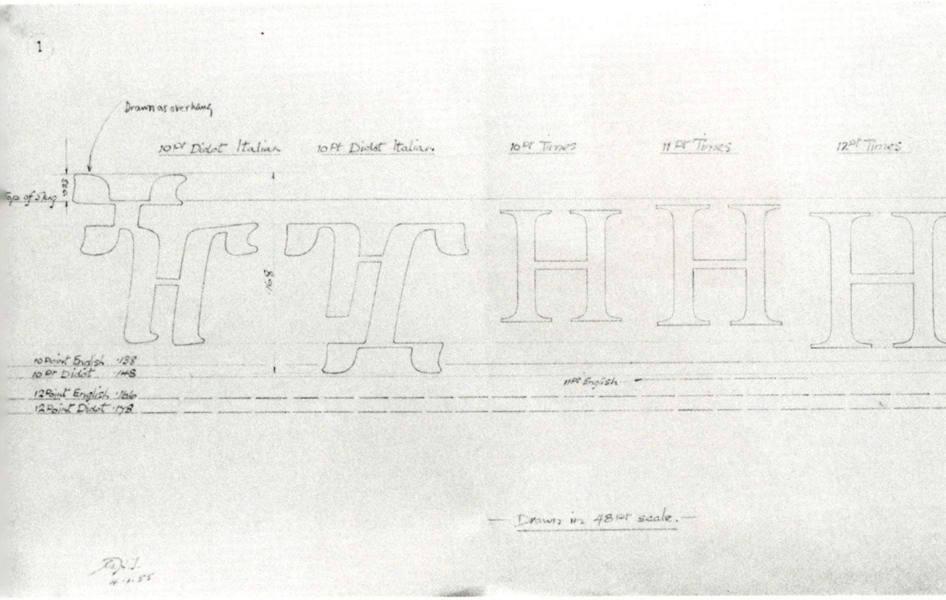

RU 27 Amharic letterforms and information sent to Walter Tracy, 1949.

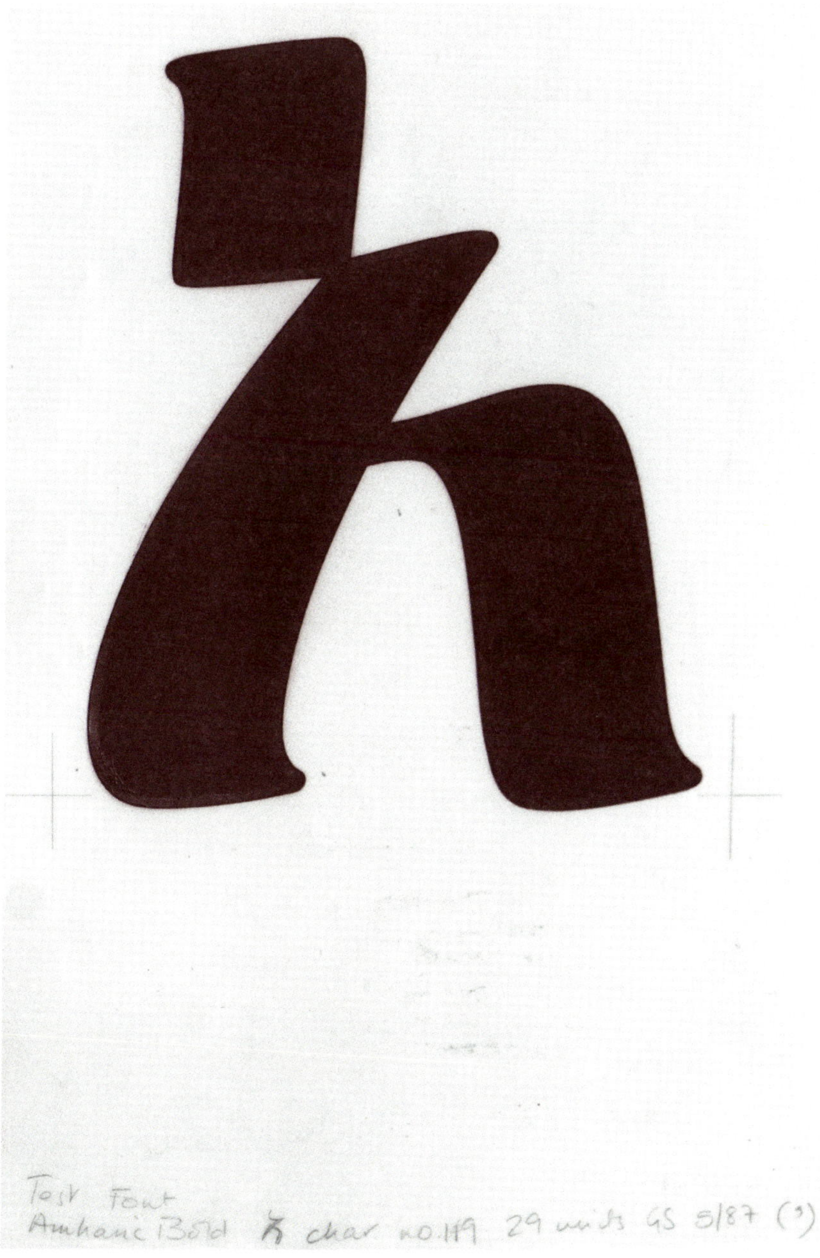

RU **28** Amharic letter-drawing for digital fonts, 1987.

RU 29 Nazanin Bold finished artwork for digital fonts showing joining forms and typically Farsi-shaped counters, *c* 1986.

RU 30 Comparative dimensions of Arabic typesetting, *c* 1977.

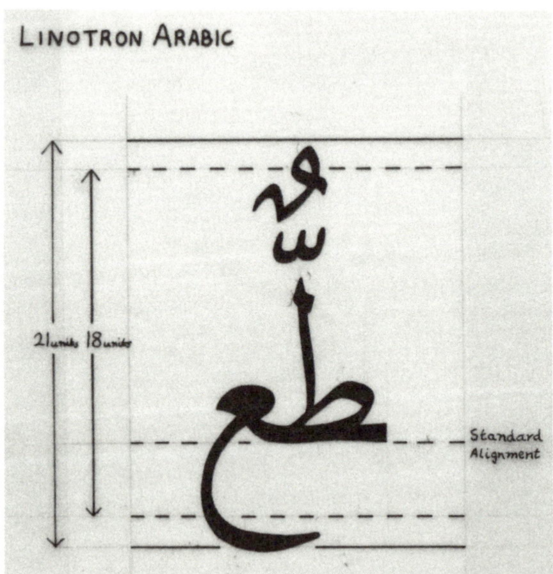

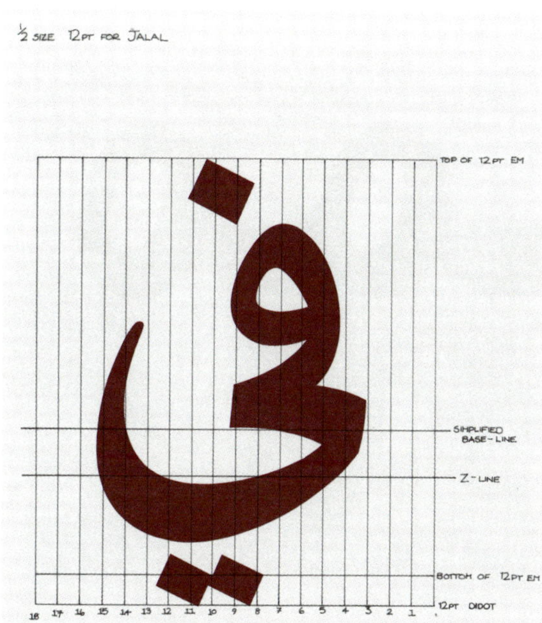

RU **31** Jalal Bold 'opaqued' letter-drawing overlaid on mask using 54-unit grid system with vertical offset for digitization, 1986.

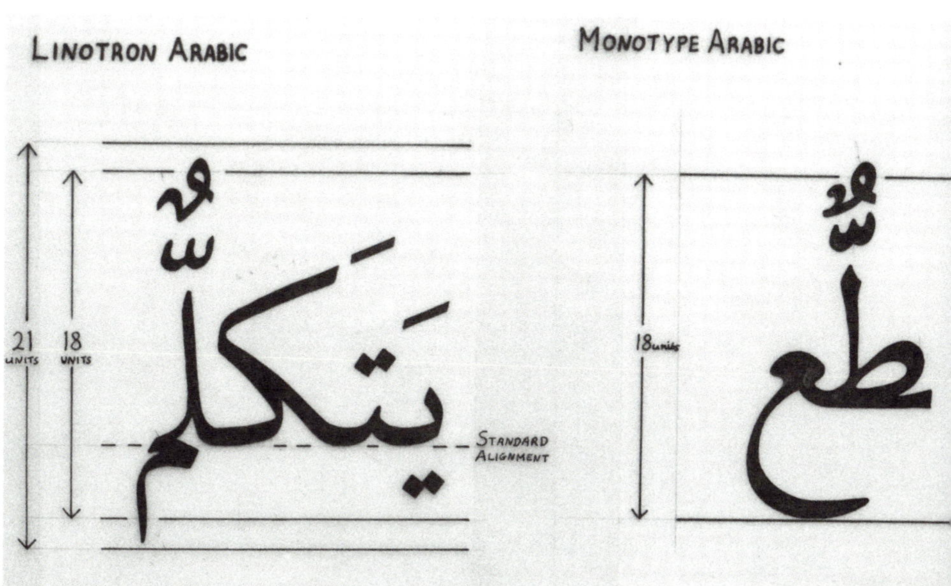

RU 32 Penned forms for Linotype Nasta'liq (Sheeraz and revision renamed Qalmi) by Tim Holloway, *c* 1987.

RU 33 Lotus Bold Urdu Naskh ligature with vertical offset, 1986.

Detail from a Tibetan astrological chart, early twentieth-century [courtesy Fiona Ross].